CANADIAN ANIMALS ARE

SMARTER THAN JACK®1

CANADIAN ANIMALS ARE

SMARTER THAN JACK®1

91 true stories

You'll see animals quite differently

The publisher
SMARTER than JACK Limited (a subsidiary of Avocado Press Limited)
PO Box 819
Tottenham
Ontario LOG 1W0
Canada
info@smarterthanjack.com
www.smarterthanjack.com

The creators
Text layout: Dominic Hurley
Cover design: DNA Designed Communications Limited
Cover photograph: © Rachael Hale Photography (NZ) Ltd 2004. All rights reserved.
Rachael Hale is a registered trademark of Rachael Hale Photography Limited.
Creator of SMARTER than JACK® medal: Simon Cosgrove
Story typing: Tina Neale and Hayley Stent
Unattributed stories: Dene Findlay and Hayley Stent
Proofreading: Vicki Andrews
Administration: Hayley Stent
Printer: Dollco
Compiler: Jenny Campbell

The distributors
Humane society partner: Canadian Federation of Humane Societies
Distributor in Canada: Publishers Group Canada
Distributor in Australia: Wakefield Press
Distributor in New Zealand: Addenda
Distributor in the United Kingdom: Airlift Book Company

The legal details
Printed in Canada
First published 2004
ISBN 0-9582457-6-2
SMARTER than JACK® is the registered trademark of Avocado Press Limited
Copyright © 2004 Avocado Press Limited

Contents

Thanks to you!

This book really belongs to everyone who has known or read about a smart animal. Many talented and generous people have had a hand in its creation.

This includes everyone who submitted a story, and especially those who had a story selected as this provided the content for this inspiring book. The people who gave us constructive feedback on earlier books and cover design, and those who participated in our research, helped us make this book even better.

The team at the Canadian Federation of Humane Societies and its participating member societies were keen to be involved, and assisted us greatly. The CFHS as well as the media, helped to get the need for stories and the book known.

Elissa Lansdell wrote the thought-provoking foreword, DNA Designed Communications Limited designed the cover, Rachael Hale Photography Limited provided the beautiful cover photograph, Simon Cosgrove designed our new SMARTER than JACK medal, Dene Findlay and Hayley Stent wrote some fabulous stories in Chapter 6, Hayley Stent helped co-ordinate all the entries, Vicki Andrews did the proofreading and Dominic Hurley did the typesetting.

Thanks to bookstores for making this book widely available to our readers, and thanks to readers for purchasing this book and for enjoying it and for giving it to others as gifts.

Lastly, I cannot forget my endearing companion, Ford the cat. Ford is now 11 years old and has been by my side all the way through the inspiring SMARTER than JACK journey.

Jenny Campbell
Creator of SMARTER than JACK

Creating your SMARTER than JACK®

Canadian animals are SMARTER than JACK®1 is a heart-warming book of tales about truly smart animals. You'll be amazed at their heroic and sometimes hilarious antics. Perhaps you've seen a cat lay the blame on an unsuspecting mate, a deer save its drowning companion or a mother skunk go to people for help when her young are in trouble!

In this book you'll read these and many other true stories about smart animals. You'll start to wonder what's really going on inside their heads.

Earlier this year people throughout Canada submitted their stories. The best were selected for this first North American edition in the SMARTER than JACK series.

There are stories about bears, skunks, porcupines, cats, dogs, otters, horses, cows, mice, deer, raccoons, elk, moose, squirrels, rabbits and an array of birds.

Profit from sales will help the Canadian Federation of Humane Societies and its participating member societies in their admirable quest to improve animal welfare.

Since 2002 the popular best-selling SMARTER than JACK series has helped raise the equivalent of us$105,000 with the first three books. The first two New Zealand editions were created in partnership with the Royal New Zealand SPCA, and the first Australian edition was created in partnership with RSPCA Australia.

The future of the SMARTER than JACK series holds a number of exciting books, with new 'country' editions, including the United Kingdom, and new editions about various types of smart animals including cats and dogs.

If you've had an amazing encounter with a smart animal we'd love to read about it. You may also like to sign up to receive the SMARTER than JACK Story of the Week for a bit of inspiration. And don't forget about the free SMARTER than JACK gift pack. See the back of this book for more details or visit www.smarterthanjack.com.

We hope you enjoy **Canadian animals are SMARTER than JACK®1** – and we hope that many animals and people benefit from it.

Foreword: *Sniffing hedges*

It was an early summer day, warm and sunny, and I had things to do.

Mojo, Surrey and I went out for a quick walk and a piddle (them, not me) so that I could take off to run some errands. They walked me (as they always do) along the nature path behind the sea of newly built houses, one of which I had moved into a few months before. Mojo had a smile on his face and that little bounce that he gets when he's outside, sniffing away at hedges and tree trunks. Surrey was pulling in the opposite direction on her extenda-leash, fascinated with something – likely a squirrel or discarded picnic sandwich.

As they sniffed, I stared into space and pondered the ever growing list of things I needed to accomplish that day: wedding plans, interview research, housework, bill payments, dry-cleaning . . . Absently, and with mild annoyance, I gave a little tug on their leash and said, 'Come on guys, we've gotta go.' They hear me say it about 100 times a walk. And about 99 of those times they pay me no attention at all. This was one of those times.

'Come on guys,' I started again, picking up my pace. 'We've gotta go!' They each stopped what they were doing for a brief second to look at me like I had two heads, and went back to sniffing.

And then it hit me.

I suddenly saw their little world through doggy eyes: a cloudless sky, leaves coming into sharp focus, the smell of blossoms from a neighbouring yard hitting me like a ton of biscuits. For the first time that day (that summer?) I could hear the chorus of birds providing our soundtrack. These dogs knew more about living than I did! What's life for, if not for getting right in there and sniffing the hedges?

This wasn't the first time I'd realized I'd been outsmarted by a four-legged companion. It would take me this entire book to list every instance, but here's a memorable one.

Our poodle Holly ruled the house for almost 18 years. Holly was middle-aged and I was 12 when we moved. Holly didn't take kindly to the change. She wanted to go back to our little town house, so much so that she tore the curtains to shreds in her efforts to escape. Dad's solution: get a cage for her to stay in when we're out. I cried fat tears, I screamed, I stomped, but Dad wasn't going to back down.

He didn't know it then, but neither was Holly.

Day one: I tearfully placed Holly in her cage in the basement and departed. Later that evening, as we pulled up in the driveway, we saw a familiar fuzzy head at the window. Holly greeted us triumphantly at the door. An argument ensued as to whether I'd really locked her in with the latch or whether I had left the cage door ajar.

Day two: My brother's turn to do the honours. He declared the cage 'locked and loaded'. Four hours later, on our return, we found Holly's familiar form once again at the window. We were baffled, until I noticed a bump and some missing hair on Holly's snout. Could it be . . .? The lock had a latch that went round and caught with a metal pin. Could our 20 pound poodle have used her beautiful pure-bred snout and sharp pure-bred brain to unlatch this complicated contraption?

Absolutely not! Dad balked. But just in case, he quietly fetched a pair of cinder blocks to wedge against the cage. No dog was going to get the better of Dad!

Day three: The familiar mop of brown curls that greeted us at the door the next night on our return did not surprise us at all. And the cage (and cinder blocks) were officially retired. Holly returned to her place of honour at the window.

I have moved countless times since then, but my home has always

Greg Tjepkema

Elissa and friends

been a happy one, full of four-legged companions and chaos. I do not fool myself into thinking that I am the mistress of the house. They decide when I wake up, where I go on my walks and how much of my dinner is actually mine.

I am blessed to be a pet owner, and deeply honoured to be a part of this amusing and amazing journey into the minds of animals. I never cease to be surprised at their brilliance and capacity for love.

Take the time to enjoy these stories of brilliant bowsers and cunning kitties. Take a little time to see the world through their insightful little eyes. And whatever you do, don't forget to take time to stop and sniff the hedges.

Elissa Lansdell
Co-host and writer of CMT Centra

1

Smart animals solve problems

A thoughtful gasper

Shooter is a Haflinger horse that we rescued from a riding stable and is my daughter Lisa's best friend. She liked to saddle and ride him in the park near us.

One day, we had saddled up and ridden out. As we trotted along, Shooter appeared to run out of breath after a few hundred yards and would stop and gasp for breath for a minute or so before starting out again. We were quite concerned about him.

Then I looked down and realized that the girth on the saddle was so loose that he was puffing himself up and holding his breath while trotting, so that the saddle would stay on and my daughter would not fall off.

It was wonderful to realize that he had such concern for my daughter's welfare. He has been a cherished member of our family for eight years now and, even though he has arthritis and is unable to be ridden anymore, he will always have a home with us.

Diane Johansen
Langley
British Columbia

Marybeth and Rebecca Schuck

Pumpkin the dog

Irritation fixed

My sister and I have a beautiful six-year-old Australian cattle dog/ husky mix. Pumpkin is a frisky, smart little girl but also extremely sensitive. Loud noises irritate her and make her run to hide in her 'den' (actually my bedroom). Of particular distress to her is how the wind will pick up and cause a door to bang in the house.

One lazy Saturday afternoon, while attempting to take a nap, I forgot the window was open – which, as you might have guessed, caused the door to bang. Pumpkin, who had been lying sleeping on the bed, calmly climbed off and proceeded to the door. What amazed us is that she quickly analyzed how to open the door by tugging on a purse which was hanging on the handle. Once the door was open wide enough (she stood and waited to see if it banged again) she jumped back on the bed and resumed her nap.

This is a dog who is smart enough to make sure her nap goes uninterrupted!

Marybeth and Rebecca Schuck
Calgary
Alberta

Utter patience

I'd like to tell you about a mother merganser whom I stood and watched while on my early morning walk.

She was a busy little mother with six little ones, and was trying to get over the boards of the dam in Bala to go from Muskoka Lake to the Moon River. She was so patient, encouraging the chicks to make the climb from the water to the top board of the dam and leap from there to the rocks below.

Obviously the chicks were instructed to wait there, as they huddled together while she went back to encourage the stragglers. You could almost hear her telling them they could do it.

When the whole family was gathered on the rock, mother waded into the tumbling waters with her little brood behind her and they bobbed their way down the falls to the river below. Such a caring mother, floating downriver, sometimes with one or two young on her back.

No human could have shown any more patience than she did at keeping her family together.

A delightful peek into life in the wild.

Marilyn Scott
Gravenhurst
Ontario

Two and two

I will begin by giving you a little background about our canine son.

One of my husband's co-workers (Gail) is involved with Doberman Rescue, and when we lived in Nova Scotia she would call us from Ontario to update us about a particular Doberman that was up for adoption at the Ottawa-Carleton Humane Society. He had been languishing in his kennel for a month or so and was slated for euthanasia since no one had expressed any interest in him. He didn't present well to would-be adopters as he barked constantly, jumped up on the kennel door and was a complete menace on a leash.

Gail then called to say that all of the breed rescues were full and could not take him and he would be euthanized the following day. I worked at the SPCA in Nova Scotia at the time and was all too familiar with that scenario, and as always I felt bad about his circumstances.

I had no intention of adopting a dog at that point, let alone a Doberman that I hadn't even seen! My husband (Marshall) told Gail we
would think about it and get back to her. Six months earlier we had
lost our 11-year-old boxer Bosley to cancer and we just weren't ready
for another dog, especially not a three-year-old Doberman with issues.

Marshall and I agreed that the timing just wasn't right and he called
her back. To my amazement he said, 'Well, Gail, I guess we're gonna
come and get him!' My jaw dropped, and the next thing I knew we
were in the van driving to Montreal to meet a volunteer from a rescue
group who had driven the dog there from Ottawa. The volunteer
opened up the dog's crate and a skinny, dull-looking Doberman
emerged. I grasped his leash and he immediately took me across the
field, apparently oblivious to the fact that I was attached! Anyway, the
rest of that adventure is a whole other story.

The dog's original name was Drakkar, but upon arrival at our home
it was quickly changed to a more appropriate handle, 'Kaos'! The cats
were completely traumatized, not because he went after them but just
because he was so loud and out of control. Many times over the
course of the ensuing months we thought we had made a terrible
mistake and contemplated having him euthanized (and I'm a firm
believer that pets are for life!). Not only did he have severe behav-
ioural problems but he also had a mysterious bleeding disorder at the
tips of his ears, and a cure was (and still is) yet to be found. We have
learned to live with blood-splattered walls, furniture, clothing, etc. His
diet also had to be modified to prevent him from vomiting at every
meal. Despite all of this we persevered.

About a year later we moved to sunny Tampa, Florida, where I
worked at the Humane Society of Tampa Bay. Kaos's ears miraculously healed! His behaviour had also improved to some degree due
to constant socialization with a variety of people, dogs and places, but
he still had issues and probably always will.

Okay, now for our dog's "smart" story.

One night after we had gone to sleep, Kaos became restless, so much so that he woke us up. He kept getting off his chair (yes, he has his own chair!) and walking around the bedroom. I thought he might have to pee, so I let him out and then brought him back in and he curled up in his chair again. Several minutes later he got up and starting walking around, and we just kept telling him to go to bed as we were both half-asleep and had to get up early the next day. He continued his restless behaviour, and finally I woke up completely when I realized what he was doing.

It was a cool night and it had become cold in the house (yes, Florida gets cold sometimes). Kaos had gone to our walk-in closet, pulled a blanket off the shelf and had succeeded in dragging it over towards his chair! People have often said that dogs are not capable of reasoning but after witnessing Kaos I completely disagree. He had no prior knowledge of the existence of a blanket in that closet but somehow he put two and two together . . . it was a proud and amazing moment for us! I covered him up with the blanket he had found and he slept soundly for the rest of the night.

We now live in Ontario and I'm working at the Guelph Humane Society. Kaos's ears are acting up again, and he still has behaviour problems despite our best efforts to modify them. We've had him for four years now and we wouldn't dream of parting with him. I've owned dogs for more than 30 years but Kaos has taught me more about dog behaviour than I ever knew before. He's a brat, but he's also a goofball and a great companion.

I hope my story made you smile.

Jackie Vanderheyden
Salem
Ontario

Help on the way

One day I noticed a female evening grosbeak at our bird feeder, banging her beak back and forth against the side of the feeder tray. She seemed quite distressed and this went on for several seconds.

A male (her partner, maybe) hopped over to her, and with his beak removed a half sunflower husk which was lodged upside down in the bottom of her beak. She seemed relieved and they flew off together. It was wonderful to see such caring between these birds.

Kathy Wells
Sillikers
New Brunswick

The mighty protector

Years ago, a scruffy black kitten appeared on our doorstep. Since it was minus 30 Canadian weather, we decided to keep him overnight. The next day we attempted to find his owner but no one claimed him. Zeke became a part of our household for 17 years. A couple of years later a small orange kitten was rescued from dogs in a schoolyard. Since no one wanted him, we welcomed him into our family. Soon this cat, named Max, and Zeke became best buddies.

We moved to an acreage outside of Calgary, and here the cats were allowed to sometimes go outside. One day we were visiting neighbours at the top of our driveway. Max was close to the house, while Zeke was near us. Suddenly another neighbour's St Bernard came bolting across the yard. He gave chase to poor terrified Max.

Zeke quickly sized up the situation. Seeing his buddy in danger, Zeke immediately pursued the dog. Across the acres ran the little orange cat, the very large dog and the black cat, all running as fast as they could. It was quite a sight to see! The St Bernard finally gave a quick look over his shoulder and saw Zeke gaining on him. The dog picked up more speed and didn't stop running until he was safely on his own porch! Once Zeke could see that Max was safe, he returned to our deck to calmly sit and lick his paws!

Donna Kuffler
Cochrane
Alberta

Too hot in his fur coat

One hot, humid summer my husband and I spent as much time as we could at our trailer at Lake Huron, and we always took our white miniature poodle Benji with us. We would often put the air conditioner on during the night if it was really hot, and turn it off during the day and open all the windows in the trailer.

On a particularly hot afternoon we were sitting in the trailer reading, the windows open, when all of a sudden Benji started barking and standing up on his hind legs, turning circles and all the while looking up at the air conditioner. He kept this up until we put the air conditioner on, then he settled down and went to sleep.

Nancy Hibbert
Petrolia
Ontario

Skunk encounter

Several years ago, we lived in North Vancouver at the edge of a natural forest. In the middle of one night, our 11-year-old daughter Cherie came running up very excitedly saying, 'Mommy, Mommy, there's a

Cherie Kroll

The skunk

skunk in my window well.' I woke up abruptly and wondered 'What do you do with a skunk trapped in a window well at 4 am?' 'Don't disturb it, that's for sure,' I thought.

The window well had a three foot corrugated metal wall on three sides and the skunk could not possibly climb out on its own. I got a long rope and opened a kitchen window, which was several feet directly above the basement window well. Then I very cautiously put the rope out the kitchen window and slowly lowered it down to the skunk.

As if on cue, the skunk stood up on its hind legs and grabbed the rope with its front paws. Again with extreme caution, I raised the rope and its passenger to ground level. The skunk then scampered into the forest without leaving a trace.

Jackie Kroll
Saskatoon
Saskatchewan

Tally and the ring

My mother's comment, at the end of the whole episode, was that she was afraid to tell anyone about it, that they'd think she was crazy. My response, however, and that of everyone I of course immediately told this story to, was that that wouldn't be the perception – people who know cats and the way they fit into the grand scheme of things would understand.

It all began about six years ago when one of my cats, Remy, was diagnosed with diabetes. In the years since Remy became diabetic she needed an ever increasing level of care. She took two insulin injections a day, and in her last few months she had been prescribed a couple of types of medication, some of which had to be added to her food.

Anyone who knew my other cat, Remy's sister Tally, knew that she wasn't really a cat – in her eating habits, anyway. She was either a dog or a pig. If you put down ten bowls of food in a row Tally would move from one to another, eating everything in sight until she exploded. Remy, on the other hand, preferred to inspect her food, sniff at it a little, possibly lie down and look at it from that very interesting angle, eat a bit, dance around it for a while and leave the room. This behaviour tended to work out quite nicely for Tally, whose lurking and circling and moving-in-for-the-kill skills would put a shark to shame. And so, with Remy's need for her medication to be mixed into her food, it seemed best for Tally to go and live with my mother, temporarily – or so I thought at the time.

And so Remy and I lived a quiet life together until that moment arrived when she was no longer my carefree dancing kitten but a tired and ill little cat ready to leave this world, unable to fight anymore. That incredibly sad day came in January 1998 and I still miss her very much.

Meanwhile, back at the ranch – or, more specifically, my mother's house – Tally was living the good life at what my friends called 'Kay's Spa'. Big decisions, such as whether to have ham or tuna for lunch and which bed to nap on, were being made. I think Tally's favourite position was sitting on the back of the chesterfield while my mother ate her lunch. From that highly desirable location Tally could actually lean over and take a bite out of a sandwich – something she did more than once. However, my mother did have other things to do besides plan Tally's menus, so out she went one fall day to rake and bag leaves.

My father died more than 12 years ago, and so naturally my mother's wedding ring is very precious to her – which is why she decided to take it off and put it in her pocket while raking the leaves. For safekeeping, or so she thought. She raked and bagged leaves, she took her car out of the garage to be picked up for service and she worked in her garden. And then she discovered the ring was gone, right out of the hole she hadn't noticed in her pocket. She searched everywhere, inside and out – driveway, gardens, walkways – to no avail.

Now, my mother is a true Englishwoman and she is rather given to understatement. When she reported this loss to me that evening she said she was 'a little upset'. That translates as total hysteria in most other people. We hatched a plan that would surely offer up the ring – a plan that meant sifting, leaf by leaf, through about 17 large garden bags. No matter, it was her wedding ring. My friends made a suggestion – rent a metal detector. Brilliant! My mother began the search for such a thing and learned her always helpful neighbour Larry could get us one. My weekend was planned. Drink lots of tea and search for the proverbial needle in the haystack.

This is where Tally comes into the story. It is now a few days later, the day before the Great Garden Bag Search, and my mother is sitting on her chesterfield, eating a sandwich, but Tally isn't on the back trying to take a bite. Tally is sitting quietly on the floor by my mother's feet, with her front paws together – the way cats often have them when they sit quietly. She looked up at my mother with a face that said *Well, you've been looking for this and I've found it for you.* And in front of her paws was the ring.

We have a theory about how this happened. It involves the ring falling from the pocket into a seam in the removable car seat . . . which was moved into the house and placed on a chair . . . on which the cat, needing to sit on a new thing as cats must, probably found the ring. And the ring – being shiny and golden and wonderful – would have been of great interest to a cat, perfect to play with and bat around the house – miraculously missing hot air registers and cracks in the hardwood – until it landed on the carpet by my mother's feet, aided by those little paws. Or maybe that's not how it happened at all.

As I said at the beginning, my mother was astounded and disbelieving, but not for long. And she and Tally, in that moment, became well and truly bonded. So, in some ways, I lost both of my cats. But I don't begrudge losing Tally for a second: she gave my mother back something very precious – and gave me a wonderful story to tell.

Hilary Kenyon
Newmarket
Ontario

Red the squirrel

It was Good Friday the day my little biddy buddy bought it – a child of nature in the shape of a red squirrel. I called him 'Red', which I know shows a startling lack of imagination, but I didn't feel I had the right to be creative, not having his ownership papers. I once had a cat I named 'Cat', only because he came with the apartment I rented while attending the University of Manitoba and I was certain he already had a name. But that's another story. Anyway, Red was the source of many smiles and laughs during a long and lonely winter of self-imposed isolation.

In December I had hung a swinging bird feeder from a beam under the front porch veranda to attract the chickadees, kinglets or any other birds who felt like a winter snack. I didn't realize at the time the great amount of angst and frustration it would cause Red. He tried every trick he knew and invented a few more in his quest to conquer the feeder.

While I sat working at my computer, I could watch him from the picture window as he schemed and analyzed. He would run along the railing and try to scale the corner post, only to slide back down. He would climb to the windowsill and try to scamper up the window to a lamp that would put him a mere three feet from his target. Didn't work! I could see his little brain working as he tried to solve his dilemma. *If I climb to the railing, jump to the window frame, then shinny up the wall to the lamp I could then leap the remaining three feet to dinner!* His head would move from side to side and up and down as he worked out all the possibilities.

I don't suppose he ever thought about how he could cling to a plastic swinging bird feeder or, in the unlikely event that he successfully completed his mission, how to return safely to the deck. I think he suffered from a severe case of tunnel vision.

Although he feasted daily on the grain and nuts the birds kicked off or rejected, he continued his obsession all through the winter. One day, after sweeping the snow off the deck, I leaned the push broom up against the window close to the lamp. This proved to be an accidental instrument of torture for Red as he tried time after time to scale the slippery broom handle, only to land in a heap on the deck.

I believe his most frustrating and infuriating moments came as he

Dan Blix

Red the squirrel

approached the object of his torment from above. I could hear his tiny footfalls on the roof, scampering back and forth, and see his tiny face peeking upside down from the overhang only two feet away from his tempting target. He managed the main beam and for a few promising seconds found a four-pawed grip on the corner post, a mere six inches from the feeder. It was only when he reached out a paw to swipe at or try to grip his swaying dinner that he lost his pawhold and crashed to the deck. I swear the air turned blue with rodent curses. Although I could see he was clearly losing his battle, as well as his

14

mind, he never gave up in his attempt to solve the mystery that was the bird feeder.

Red was also obsessed with me. He would sit on the wood pile just outside my window not three feet away and watch as I plunked away on my keyboard. We would stare at each other in a contest of nerves to see who would blink first. I never won! I would occasionally stare at him cross-eyed and I swear after a time he would do the same – proved, I thought, when he took an uncharacteristic tumble after taking a wrong turn on the top log.

On the occasions that my wife Linda and our crazy standard poodle Taja would visit from the city, Red would lose all interest in me in an attempt to bend Taja's brain a little further. He would tease her mercilessly, at one point even running between her legs.

Needless to say, Red and I became friends over the winter and early spring.

It was in the early afternoon of Good Friday, as I went to fill my cleaning bucket from the rain barrel, that I discovered Red face down and lifeless in the water. I felt terrible and sad as I lifted him out by the tail. I felt responsible for not having had the foresight to cover the barrel against such a happening. Shortly afterwards I left for a visit in the city, knowing that when I returned on Easter Sunday I would not be greeted by my furry little winter jester.

Given the significance of the day of Red's departure, and as one of God's creatures, I somewhat expect a visit to my wood pile by an albino squirrel with large crossed eyes, buck teeth and a halo who just may, finally, have a solution to the bird feeder puzzle.

Dan Blix
Loon Lake
Ontario

2

Smart animals know where to get help

True loyalty

During the 'dirty thirties', my parents used horses to work their Manitoba farm. Our favourite team was a matched pair of big gentle Belgians.

One Sunday, all the horses had been turned out to pasture in a distant field, so I was startled when I heard a horse neighing and stamping in the yard. The big gelding was there alone, and as he would never leave his mate I knew she must be in some kind of trouble.

Whickering at me to hurry, he led me at a fast pace through brush and small trees to where the mare was caught in a tangle of a broken-down barbed wire fence. As I worked to free her, her mate stood nearby whickering encouragement and 'bossing the job'.

Jessie Burr
Duncan
British Columbia

Trusted to help

For years we've had a birdhouse on the side of our chimney and we enjoy watching the parents feed their young from our second-storey window. Two or three broods are raised in it each summer.

One night, we were awakened by strange sounds outside. I got up to investigate and saw that a cat had climbed up the wooden edge of the chimney (not easy to do) and was trying to reach into the birdhouse to get the babies. I chased him off and went back to bed.

The next afternoon, when we were on our deck, mom and pop sparrow were sitting on the fence near our deck. They were making quite a racket. They would fly to their birdhouse with insects, only to return to the fence with their beaks still full, all the while chirping like crazy. One of the sparrows even flew to the deck railing while I was on the swing just a foot away, and sat next to me for a long time. This was very unusual.

We went to investigate, knowing that the starlings sometimes try to destroy their nest. Nothing appeared to be wrong, so I got the ladder and went up for a closer look. It turned out that the cat had reached into the birdhouse and had pulled at the straw inside, thereby flipping the nest and trapping the babies under the straw.

All that morning, the parents could hear their young in there but couldn't reach them to feed them. I opened the birdhouse and, as I took each baby out (they were only about a week old), the parents sat quietly, watching me from the roof next door, until I put the nest back together, placed the babies back in and left. The parents immediately resumed feeding their young.

Mom and pop sparrow somehow felt we could be trusted and came to us for help. Probably born in that birdhouse, they were used to us being in the garden, filling the bird feeder and chasing away those pesky starlings from their house every year. We've since moved the birdhouse beyond the reach of any more athletic cats.

Alec Boucher
Kanata
Ontario

Donna Deacon

Jake the dog

He's a hero to me

Sure, our dog Jake is smart, but it's his compassion and caring that really make him a hero in my eyes. This is the story of how Jake, an eight-year-old collie/husky cross, saved our elderly black Lab Jewel from a night of anxiety and injury.

Recently, my husband David was away on a business trip, leaving our two dogs and me to fend for ourselves. One night, after letting the dogs in after a final run around the garden, I said goodnight, turned off the lights and went upstairs. A few minutes later, while I was reading in bed, I heard Jake whining outside my bedroom door.

Although Jake is pretty attached to me, it was out of character for him to make a fuss at bedtime. For a moment I thought maybe he was just missing David. I called to him through the door, 'Jake, it's time to settle down and go to sleep.' His whining only became more agitated, and when he began to scratch at the door I just knew something must be wrong.

As I opened the door, there he was, circling around and obviously wanting something. I reached out to calm him but he backed away towards the stairs. Suddenly, I realized he wanted me to follow him. 'This can't be happening,' I thought, 'it's like something out of a Lassie movie.' That's when I heard whimpering coming from downstairs. Jake ran ahead of me as I took the stairs two at a time.

There was Jewel, in her bed, with one toenail (the dew claw) hooked in the metal ring of her collar, unable to get up or release her foot. She looked so frightened and upset. Jake sniffed her face and stayed close by as I unhooked her claw and took off the collar. As I soothed Jewel, I reached out for Jake's furry neck and just sat there on the floor holding both of them while my heart rate slowed back to normal.

At first, I couldn't believe Jake had actually come to get me when Jewel was in distress, but the more I thought about it, the more I reflected how intuitive and caring dogs can be. I shudder when I think of how easily our old Jewel could have seriously hurt herself trying to stand up. Then I hug Jake and thank him for being there when he was needed.

Donna Deacon
Langley
British Columbia

The unfortunate lookalike

We adopted a wee dog of mixed terrier breeding. We live on a ranch and have six cats. One of them is black with long hair and green eyes, named Jasper. Our dog, named Chasi, gets along fine with all of our cats, as she grew up with them.

One day I was sitting working on the computer and I could hear Chasi barking this funny high-pitched bark. I could hear a cat meowing. I ran out the front door and saw Jasper meowing at the dog, and Chasi barking at the cat and then at me. I thought Chasi was learning to chase the cats, and chastised her for it.

Well, several days later it happened again. This time my husband was home to witness it and he, too, tried to get Chasi to stop barking. But to no avail. So I went outside to grab Chasi and bring her into the house so that Jasper could get some peace. As I walked outside and down the steps I saw Jasper, Bandit and Sophia sitting there on the deck, sunning themselves.

I looked at the black cat Chasi was barking at, and it was actually a black cat that looked just like Jasper! I grabbed Chasi and put her into the house. Then I coaxed the poor cat over and noticed that he had been tearing the hair out of his neck and had several long cuts behind his ears. The poor cat was in need of immediate veterinary care. We captured him and took him to the vet.

How did my little dog know the difference between Jasper and this strange cat and know that it needed help? I have learned a very valuable lesson. I know to listen to my animals. They are smarter than me!

Sandi Good
High River
Alberta

The payback

Petra, one of 36 Lhasa Apsos seized from a suspected puppy mill by the Port Alberni SPCA in January 2004, has more than repaid her debt to the loving guardian who adopted her.

Earlier this month Petra's new 'mom', Anne Porter of Port Alberni, was watching television with her new dog by her side when Petra suddenly began barking loudly and racing back and forth across the house. The extreme agitation was completely out of character for the gentle little dog.

When Porter went to investigate she discovered that a fire had broken out in her laundry room and had quickly spread. The Port Alberni Fire Department arrived on the scene and managed to extinguish the blaze, but they told Porter that if Petra hadn't alerted her to the fire the outcome would have been much, much worse.

And so, too, would Petra's fate have been if she hadn't been rescued from the puppy mill, where she was found near death from starvation, flea-infested and covered in excrement. A few weeks longer, and she could easily have become just another one of the hundreds of animals who suffer and die each year at the hands of cruel or negligent guardians.

Charges of animal cruelty were proved against Petra's former guardians after an SPCA investigation, and Petra is basking in her new role as hero in her adopted home.

Lorie Chortyk, British Columbia SPCA
Vancouver
British Columbia

A tiny life

When we first met our then very pregnant Nimbus, a beautiful black feline with a friendly, loving disposition, we knew instinctively she was very special.

Within a few weeks of giving birth to her six little bundles of fluff, we learned just how special. Prior to becoming our cat, Nimbus visited other homes in the neighbourhood, especially our neighbour two houses down. While we were willing to supply a comfortable birthing area, she opted instead to have her kittens in this neighbour's carport – in a blue tarp piled in the corner. She and her family shared a rather cramped space with two cars and so we decided to move them, with the neighbour's blessing, to a straw bale enclosure in our backyard.

The bales were low enough for Nimbus to jump in and out of, but not for her youngsters to do likewise. We were concerned that one of Nimbus' kittens – a silver tabby we named Goliath – was particularly tiny, and gave him special attention to try and help him develop at the same rate as the other kittens.

All seemed to be going well, until one morning our neighbour knocked on our door very early to let us know that Nimbus and an unconscious kitten were at his place. Rushing there we found Nimbus standing over her very tiny Goliath.

Nimbus, realizing Goliath was very ill, knew she had to get help for her kitten and had picked him up, jumped out of the straw enclosure with him, and carried him across an empty lot and two other yards to take her kitten to the neighbour. She knew he rose earlier than us from her daily visits to his house before and after her kittens were born. She then waited by the carport door for the neighbour to come out and find her little Goliath and help him.

Sadly, despite the best efforts of our local veterinarian and his assistants, Goliath died the next day. We will never forget the incredible intelligence, maternal instinct and determination shown by our Nimbus as she tried her best to save her tiny kitten.

Gordon Hardy
Dresden
Ontario

Raspberry to the rescue

Our family had a beagle/Lab cross named Raspberry – her name is another story altogether!

One summer afternoon, Raspberry returned from roaming, breathing heavily and obviously excited. One of our sons was in the yard. She ran up to him, then ran away, ran back, then ran away, until he realized he was to follow her.

Dashing off, she led him to a thicket where a mother cat lay with a number of newborn kittens. The mother was apparently ill and in some distress, and might have died without some intervention.

A passer-by was hailed. Fortunately, he recognized the cat and the owners were contacted. We have always believed that Raspberry's quick action saved not only the mother cat but the wee kittens as well.

Yeah! Raspberry!

Ted and Arlene Kropp
Abbotsford
British Columbia

Faithful old friend

A mop with legs. That is how we frequently describe our elderly little Lhasa Apso dog, Spike.

In his younger years, Spike and my husband Len were inseparable. Then our lives changed forever when my husband was diagnosed with the dreaded disease of Alzheimer's. Spike became increasingly protective of his pal as time went on. The little dog seemed to realize that his special person needed extra attention as Len's memory faded to include only his distant past.

One hot summer evening at our cottage, after an exhausting day, I stretched out on the couch for a few minutes of rest, but promptly fell asleep. Within a short time, Spike arrived at the door and gave one loud and very sharp bark. I instantly came to attention . . . this was not Spike's usual kind of bark. He didn't want in the cottage, and Len was nowhere to be seen . . . also unusual.

Spike started up the long wooded lane, but kept looking back at me. Uncertain, I paused on the deck. Spike gave another sharp bark and continued up the lane. By then I realized that Len must be lost or in some other kind of difficulty, and faithful little Spike had decided to go for help.

Within five or ten minutes, Spike led me right to Len's side. He was wandering around in a state of confusion, lost among the trees. Spike and I assisted Len back to the cottage, thus averting a crisis.

Len passed from this earth four years ago, and Spike, at age 14, is now in his golden years. The spring is gone from his step, his eyes are clouded with cataracts and his hearing is fading. We realize that Spike's days are numbered, and probably before long our little dog will be going to doggy heaven, but we will always remember Spike as our hero for the day he rescued Len.

Elva Avery
Moncton
New Brunswick

Help me please!

This incident happened a few years ago in North Vancouver. I had been out for dinner with my wife and children and arrived home about midnight. I heard a knock on the back door, which surprised me since our backyard was not accessible from the street.

I opened the back door to see a raccoon standing on the porch. I went back inside, only to hear a knock on the door again. The raccoon still stood there and was the obvious source of the knock. This time she walked part-way down the stairs, stopped and looked back as if waiting for me to follow . . . so I did. The raccoon walked ahead and stopped, and again waited for me to follow. Slowly, she led me to the fence and into our neighbour's backyard.

There, I discovered that the racoon's little babies had tumbled into my neighbour's drained swimming pool. I got a long board and placed it into the pool so that mama racoon could gain entry into the pool and reach her babies. She carried each of her babies out to safety, one at a time. Once she had accomplished this, she looked back at me as if to say *Thank you* and then went off on her merry way, family in tow.

An amazing story of animal intelligence.

Don Smith
Chilliwack
British Columbia

A skunk in a jam

We live in a small quaint town in rural Ontario. A mother skunk decided to make her nest in a mound of earth beside our home. We would see mama skunk and her baby skunks out for their waddles from time to time. No one on our street dared go near them for fear of being sprayed!

One day my 15-year-old daughter was in the backyard when she spotted mama skunk waddling around lopsided. She appeared to be stuck and unable to free herself. On closer inspection my daughter noticed that mama had a jar stuck on her head!

Without hesitation my daughter started toward mama skunk. Our neighbours watched in fascination as she got closer and closer to mama skunk. All eyes were on them! My daughter grabbed hold of that jar with both hands and pulled! Mama's head popped out! With a nod of her head mama turned and waddled away.

Not a raised tail or a spray that day – just one girl helping another out of a jam! A jar of jam, that is!

Kim Lopes
Almonte
Ontario

A will to survive

A special heifer calf was born in Louis Creek, BC on February 28, 2004 at the Mountain Meadows Ranch. What makes this calf special? Her mother is a survivor of the McLure/Barriere wildfire.

When Louis Creek was swept by wildfire on August 1, 2003, ranchers Bob and Jill Hayward evacuated as many cattle as could be rounded up from the crown range on the mountain behind their ranch. Unfortunately, 17 cows and calves were left behind.

'It was terrible to know that we couldn't get them all off the mountain in time,' says Jill Hayward. 'Knowing they had no escape from the fire left us all feeling sick.'

The Haywards returned to their ranch eight days after the fire, and were finally able to clear trails up to the range approximately ten days later.

'Nothing remained up there,' said Bob Hayward, 'just total devastation of the forest and meadows, with everything blackened and turned into ash and no sign of surviving cattle.'

Six weeks after the fire, Jill Hayward returned home from work to find two cows sleeping in the driveway of the ranch. One cow was the Haywards' and one belonged to Bill Matuga of Vinsulla. Both cows had lost their calves and were extremely thin. The Haywards' cow, Reba, was severely burned in several areas including her hooves and udder.

'The cow's biggest problem was depression, she acted like she needed Prozac. Obviously her experience in the fire had left her damaged both physically and mentally,' stated Jill Hayward.

Special care and medical treatment for Reba have proved their worth. Almost all the burns are healed and the arrival of her 2004 calf has put her into happy mother mode again, say the Haywards. Even the burned udder is working just fine on all four faucets.

'We know Reba is not worth much at today's market prices, but she is truly special to have the smarts to survive the wildfire and to have walked out of the devastation on that mountain,' says Jill Hayward. 'Her will to survive and carry on has earned her a special place in our hearts.'

Article by Jill Hayward
Louis Creek
British Columbia

Gypsy knows best

It's a well-known fact that, when horses are travelling in a herd, individual animals do not leave the safety of the group. It takes intelligence to know when it is better to leave this place of safety to seek help elsewhere.

While working around the barn one hot summer afternoon, the owners of the riding stable where we boarded our horses noticed two of the animals moving away from the herd, which was grazing at the far end of the 30 acre field in which they were enclosed. Slowly the horses worked their way toward the barn, and as the people watched they began to realize that one of their mares, Roxy, was being driven toward the stable by my three-quarter thoroughbred mare, Gypsy.

Roxy was clearly reluctant to leave the herd, constantly turning back or stopping completely. Gypsy was, by turns, leading Roxy or moving in behind to nip at her rump to keep her heading in the direction of the stable. As the horses neared, the owners opened the gate and went into the field to meet them and take Roxy's halter. Immediately they had hold of Roxy, Gypsy turned and trotted back to the herd. The owners, thoroughly puzzled by now, began checking over the mare, and soon discovered a severed artery in her pastern. Had she stayed with the herd she would quickly have bled to death.

Thanks to an intelligent decision made by another horse, Roxy was cared for and lived for many years.

Eleanor Westgate
London
Ontario

3

Smart animals teach us lessons

'I've got my own!'

I have a beagle called Maggie who becomes as excited as any pre-school child at Christmas time.

One recent Christmas my husband and I were lying in bed, with the trusty beagle curled up in her usual spot at our feet, when our son came in from his Christmas party. He came into the room to show us the stocking full of presents that he had received from his secret Santa.

Maggie was immediately excited with a little extra Christmas hype and started jumping and nipping at the bright red stocking that our son was holding. Each time she would jump for it he calmly lifted it out of her reach and continued to pull his gifts out to show us. Disgruntled in the way only a beagle can be, she jumped down off the bed and headed out of the room for what we thought would be a regular beagle sulk.

Less than two minutes later she came bolting into the room carrying her Christmas stocking, which was exactly the same stocking that our son was holding. She had gone to the basement into a box of old Christmas decorations and retrieved her old red stocking that had been stored away since the previous year. I know I would have trouble

Virdell Barclay

Maggie the dog

putting my finger on that stocking and she managed to find it in less than two minutes.

Virdell Barclay
Okotoks
Alberta

The Chief

'He's not normal!' was the general assessment at our house. 'He's all mixed up!'; 'He'll never be worth anything'; 'Face it, he's useless!' This was our father's assessment of our friend.

In a farming situation, where animals' worth is judged either by the pound or by their ability to work, it seemed that this one had nothing to offer – nothing, that is, but his friendly personality, his unflagging good humour and his often-expressed love of life, his *joie de vivre*.

He had come accidentally into this world, unwanted and resented, a mongrel born into a family with a long and cherished pedigree. He had been welcomed into our family delightedly by us children and with long-suffering, duty-bound sighs from our parents.

We called him the Chief, and he grew the long-legged elegant frame of his Irish setter mother and the black and white coat and markings of his border collie father – our cattle dog. Witnesses gave indisputable evidence of his paternity, prompting our parents to offer a home to one of the offspring.

He spent his first five months frolicking and growing, unencumbered by responsibilities, until his size and speed prompted our father to begin his training as a cattle dog. His hope was that genetics would pay off and that some of the formidable cattle abilities of the pup's father would be present in the Chief – and that the mother's bird dog inclinations would miraculously be absent from his genes.

Every day, Chief was taken to the pastures to study his intended craft. Our father became less and less impressed with his charge, eventually laughing hopelessly when asked about his progress. Finally, we were taken to the fields for a display of the Chief's progress. Dancing around our father, Chief eagerly awaited the command which would send him out over the knoll to the far side of the pasture where the cattle could be seen. We smiled as he streaked across the field, over the knoll and out of our view. As we watched, the cattle continued to graze peacefully, a few of the closer ones lifting their heads momentarily before continuing with their grazing. Minutes passed and we asked where Chief was.

'This you have to see' was our answer as we began to walk to the knoll over which the dog had disappeared. Soon, while the cattle grazed contentedly, we could see the source of our father's frustration, motionless, head up, tail straight behind him, in a perfect Irish setter field dog stance, eyes fixed on the cattle. Laughing, our father shouted 'I know where they are! Go get them!' And to us, 'What do I have to do – shoot one?'

Mildred Drost, DVM
Riverbank
New Brunswick

The correct assessment

My father was a farmer and stockman in Saskatchewan with many years of practical experience. He was a natural with animals of all kinds, and in the absence of a nearby veterinarian, and probably of the money to pay for such services, he became adept at dealing with crises.

Our dog Nicky, a collie/terrier cross, at about middle age, broke his leg. Dad splinted it with small strips of wood and cotton wrappings. Nicky ran happily on three legs for some days and then removed the splints. Dad felt the leg was not sufficiently healed so he gathered the discarded splints and again attached them to the dog's limb. Nicky didn't agree with this diagnosis and a short time later again removed the splints. After Dad had repeated this operation twice, he watched Nicky remove the splints then dig a hole in the ground and bury the offending objects.

The leg healed beautifully and Dad concluded that Nicky's assessment was the correct one.

Patricia Grant
Edmonton
Alberta

Shh . . . I'm trying to sleep!

I have many hobbies that I enjoy. I love to rollerblade, I've played volleyball since I was 12, I have a Leonard Maltin passion for the movies, I volunteer at my local humane society and, if I didn't think it would bring me public ridicule and the same contempt afforded mimes, I would admit to being a mascot. My husband Dave and I are both avid golfers and we hit the links whenever we can.

All of the above strenuous activities lead to my favourite pastime of all . . . sleeping. If you were to call my home at 9.30 in the evening, I'd already have been in bed for half an hour. If the phone rings past 10 pm or before 10 am, I automatically expect that it is the police calling to impart bad news, or my pesky older brother phoning to ask 'Are you already in bed/Are you still in bed?' even though he has been getting the same shrieking answer for 20 years.

It is a wonder, then, why I acquired a Labrador . . . a breed whose hobbies include competing in high jump, long jump, hurdles, sprints, long distance running and swimming. Owning a Labrador is like operating a blender without a lid and you're trying to stop the mess by covering it with a dime. I should have taken my lifestyle into consideration and adopted a three-toed sloth who sleeps an average of 23 hours a day.

As you know, dogs are creatures of habit and they do not like their routine to be broken or adjusted. From Monday to Friday, Newman,

Dave and I have a ritual that we go through every morning which works well and keeps us all on schedule. Well, by Newman's schedule I mean sleeping, eating, barking at Wally through the baby gate and eating his way through the laundry room wall. I think he has seen *The Shawshank Redemption* one too many times and one day I'll come home to find a tunnel that led him to freedom and a tropical island.

What Newman is NOT accustomed to is weekends and the concept of sleeping in. I've tried to keep him up late on Friday and Saturday nights by watching *Homeward Bound, K9* or *All Dogs Go to Heaven* and I've even sat him down and pointed out the calendar to him. But so far the only thing he has duly noted are the major food holidays (Christmas, Easter and Thanksgiving) and what date *101 Dalmatians* will be released on DVD with bonus blooper footage. So, like an alarm clock, Newman still dutifully awakens on Saturdays and Sundays at 6 am to let us know that it's time to shower. I think you know what I'm talking about when I describe the manner in which he 'lets us know'.

I would imagine that in some households you are awakened when a soaring, shaggy 90 pound caber lands on your solar plexus. In other households it's a little less painful, as if in a dream where your feet are being washed by a buffalo's tongue. In our household, Newman is not allowed on the bed, so his tactics are a little more subtle. For whatever reason, I am always Newman's target in the mornings. Personally, I think he and Dave have some sort of unanimous consensus that I am to blame for the neutering and will pay for it dearly until the end of time or until said baubles are returned to their original geographic location.

In any event, Newman consistently picks on me. It starts with him sitting next to the bed, right at my head and staring at me. I don't even have to have my eyes open and I know he's staring at me with the penetrating gaze of Mona Lisa. I ignore this. He will then proceed to

36

snort as if he's got pepper in his snout, which I wouldn't mind so much except that he sprays my forehead with snot. I cover my head with the duvet and tell him to go lie down. Not having mastered the English language, he cocks his head at me and yawns. This in itself could almost propel me out of bed because Newman's breath usually smells like he ate a dead gopher for breakfast.

I poke my head out and tell him 'Not today, Newman, go lie down' and cover my head again. After about five seconds, what feels like a paperweight lands on my head. I haven't actually asked for his paw, and yet it has just given me a slight concussion. I ignore him further and a search and rescue mission starts. He will flip up the edge of the duvet with his nose and start to snuffle around until he finds skin, which can take some time because the comforter is covering his eyes like a wedding veil and he can't see a thing. At this juncture I poke my nose out from my hiding space and laughingly tell him to knock it off. His response is to launder my face with saliva and start thumping his tail on the side of the bed like some crazed percussionist.

One command that Newman does comprehend is 'Where's Dave?' whereupon he will frantically explore the immediate area until he uncovers said hubby. In a last desperate attempt to hit this four-legged drooling snooze button, I ask 'Where's Dave?' and he trots over to the other side of the bed. In what I am sure is a covert language, Dave whispers something in Newman's ear that translates into 'Mom had you fixed' and Newman is back in my face. I wave the white flag, which is usually Dave's Calvin Kleins strewn about the floor, and get up to begin my work day as Newman's personal assistant.

In keeping with my favourite hobby, I am also an avid napper. In truth, I wholeheartedly applaud Mexico, a country that insists on its inhabitants taking a nap every day to escape the rigours of manual labour. I can generally be found during that compulsory time frame in one of our spare rooms readying for a nap with Wally. This is a much beloved ritual I have carried over from my single days, which may explain why my single days lasted as long as Bob Hope.

I shut the door for these sacred rest periods because Newman resents the 'Dee time' that Wally is receiving and tends to walk the picket line for the bed privileges that Wally also gets. No sooner have I shut the door than the heavy breathing and snorting starts in the crack between the carpet and the bottom of the door. It's like trying to sleep while Shrek breathes through a clogged straw. When I advise Newman to 'Go away', his brain translates that into dog-ese as 'scratch all the verathane off the door'. I am now far too comfortable to actually get up and let Newman outside, so I start bellowing for Dave to 'Come and get your dog!', which I suppose he would have heard if he wasn't taking a nap on the living room couch.

Having said all this, I do get my revenge. When Newman is sound asleep, I do what all of you have done to your dogs or are sadistically waiting to do to them. I tickle the hair between the pads of his feet. There is nothing more hilarious than making your sleeping dog look as though he is riding a bicycle. Admit it, that flailing back leg makes you feel triumphant for every time he has ever blown Revelly on the proverbial trumpet. When he lifts his groggy head and looks at you with that annoyed *What are you doing?* evil eye, you can merely shrug and tell him 'Hey, it's not the weekend.'

Dee Clair
Calgary
Alberta

A dog's role

Mum and Dad and one-year-old Bren were preparing to welcome into the family their first dog. Bren was particularly interested in helping to make him a cosy box. Anticipation was high. At the appointed hour Leader's previous owners brought him to the house. A large gangling puppy with big paws, he was curious about his new home. After a moment's hesitation, the seating arrangement was soon settled – Bren curled up in the box, and Leader sat up expectantly on the sofa.

Leader soon adjusted to his new home, and continued to make his own unconventional decisions. It was wintertime and the family lived in rural Alberta. Mum had the happy plan of training Leader to pull Bren along on the sled. However, Bren was keen on pulling the sled himself, and it was Leader who enjoyed travelling on the sled. So, once again, the conventional roles were reversed.

Marjorie Meredith
North Vancouver
British Columbia

Tina knew best

Close to where I live is an animal farm. The veterinarian I worked with also happened to be the vet for this park.

One day he was called out to look at the elephant called Tina. It seemed Tina had a problem with one of her front feet. Tina was patiently waiting for the doctor when he arrived at the park.

'Hello Tina,' he said. 'Let's have a look at that sore foot, shall we?' as he patted the foot he was told he was to examine. With that, Tina lifted one of her back feet. Again the doctor patted the front foot, but Tina continued to lift the hind leg.

After several failed attempts at getting her to raise her front foot, he decided to appease her and have a look at the foot she was raising. Lo and behold, he discovered that the foot she was showing him was in worse condition than the front foot that he was called in to examine.

Who says animals are not smart? Tina certainly knew which foot hurt the most, and which one she wanted treated first!

Jillian Siddall

Perfect wake-up

When I was a teenager, we had a chocolate point Siamese named Burt. We knew he was smarter than he let on, but one day he really showed us his cards.

It was time for me to get up in the morning and go to school. However, waking a teenager always was a challenge for my mom. One day she got tired of the struggle, so she told Burt to go wake me up. At her command, Burt walked out of the kitchen and down the hall into my bedroom. He then climbed up the wooden ladder to my top bunk and proceeded to walk across the length of my body. Once he got close enough to my face, Burt ever so gently took my earlobe between his teeth and bit down, with just enough pressure to wake me up!

Beats an alarm clock any day!

Dan Hoch
Calgary
Alberta

Our boss rabbit

When my children were young we had a pet rabbit, Topaz, who lived in a room addition of our mobile trailer in British Columbia. This room also housed our wood stove and the hot-water heater.

Topaz liked to hop on top of the wood stove to get warm. Sometimes he would get very angry with us and dance a warpath around our feet demanding attention, or to have the wood stove fed if it was too cold.

If he was left alone and did not think we had spent enough time with him, he would go to the hot-water heater and turn the switch off. When we needed to have a shower or wash the dishes and the water was cold, we knew our rabbit was angry with us again.

Gloria Hockley
Whitehorse
Yukon Territory

4

Smart animals help us out

Intelligence without training

What's a dog to do to have a fun run when the owner is tired, grumpy, upset and has a sprained ankle as well? If the dog in question is an Airedale terrier, he resorts to comedy.

After a long night of arguing with my husband, lacking sleep and needing to get out of the house for a break, I took Togger for a walk to one of his favourite bush areas. This was an area just outside the city where he could run freely, hunt and pretend to be wild. Not wanting to walk too far with a sore ankle I was hobbling along, grumbling all the way, while he had his walk.

In a short while he disappeared into the bush, reappearing with a very large leaf on top of his head. This was a leaf roughly eight inches in diameter, and how he got it on the top of his head is beyond me but he did. He kept it in perfect balance as he cavorted and danced in front of me. I called him to come so I could remove the leaf from his head but he was not having any of that nonsense. He continued the silliness until I started laughing – wish I could have taken a picture! I realized that this was his intention from the start: to present such a clownish, silly picture that I would have to laugh, thus relieving some of my anger.

Airedales will take offence when laughed at but will also resort to clowning or acting silly when it suits the moment. His act changed the walk from a chore to a pleasure. He was clearly sensitive to my mood, taking charge to remedy the situation.

This is the same dog who a few months later displayed another side of his intelligence, again on a bush walk. At the end of a long walk, in order to get back to the car and avoid the road I decided to take a trail through the bush. Midway through the trail we came to an area where there were tracks and animal droppings. Being unfamiliar with the tracks and type of droppings, I got a spooky feeling – was this animal large or small, harmless or dangerous?

Turning to consult Togger, I found that he had disappeared. Nothing I could do but keep on going and hope for the best. Finally making my way to the open field, I called. He appeared on the far side of the field at the top of a ravine. Obviously, he had disappeared to track the animal to ensure it did not follow me, trusting that I could find my own way to the field. I never did find out what type of animal it was and was not tempted to investigate further. Each time we hiked in the same area he would disappear to check the situation, often changing the route I chose to avoid whatever the danger was near.

These are just two examples of the intelligence of a dog who was sold in a pet store as a Yorkshire terrier and spent the first year of his life locked in a basement because, SURPRISE, he was an Airedale terrier.

As the title of this story suggests, all this is without formal training. He has the innate intelligence for hunting and to determine my feelings and differentiate between upset and frightened, doing what is necessary to make many situations more pleasant.

Betty Hirsekorn
Edmonton
Alberta

The horse who went to school

Early one morning in the summer of 1946 my dad called me to get up quick and help him with Ginger, my school horse. Ginger was very smart, usually too smart for his own good.

During the night Ginger had unlocked the door to the cow barn and helped himself to the chop (dry food for livestock) bin. When my dad got up, Ginger had his belly full and had washed it down with water, which had made the chop expand in his stomach. At this point Ginger was lying in the middle of the yard with his legs in the air, almost dead.

Dad and I forced him to drink two quarts of linseed oil, in the hope that it would soften the chop and help save his life. We didn't think our old friend would be alive when we got home from school that day.

At approximately 11.30 am, I was in class when a loud noise was heard out on the veranda at the front of the school. The teacher asked one of the students to go to the door. To our surprise my horse had come to school. He walked up the five steps and was making a lot of noise and wiping his nose on the glass window in the door.

The student told the teacher that it was 'Smith's horse', and the teacher told me to go put my horse in the barn.

Ginger followed me to the barn and I shut him in. During dinner hour I phoned my dad and told him the horse had come to school and was in the barn. My dad didn't believe me and had to go look out the window, thinking the horse was still there. I told him that my sister and I would ride Ginger home, even though we didn't have a bit, halter, lines or even a rope to put on him.

After school we got on Ginger in the barn. The other kids opened the door for us, and we were off home. The entire three and a half mile trip home was under Ginger's control. We went between the neighbour's house and barn, up between the CNR train tracks and through a six inch high grain crop, finally stopping for him to get a drink in a slough filled with water. My sister and I were quite amused with the trip, but we were a bit scared when he decided to eat weed off the bottom of the slough; we had to lift our legs up high to keep dry, and almost slipped down his neck into the water.

A few nudges to his side got him on his way and we finally arrived home, an hour late. Our dad was waving from the upstairs barn door. All the way home Ginger was passing gas and we were awfully glad we weren't in the cart behind him as usual!

The next day was Saturday and I had to go to the school barn and sweep down all the walls, mangers and door to remove the residue of chop. My horse was a favourite with all the school kids and was known to eat anybody's unwanted lunch. He ate rhubarb pie, buns, all kinds of sandwiches and the tassel of any tuque he could steal. One of the kids in grade 5 almost got the strap because he told the teacher that Smith's horse was smarter than her!

Cecil F Smith
Moose Jaw
Saskatchewan

Villains meet Brigadier

Nearly 15 years ago we acquired a largish dog, who turned out to be a bearded collie cross, and called him Brigadier – Brig for short. The story of his young life was not a happy one. He was a pet shop puppy from who knows where, given to a child as a Christmas present. But it seemed that no one had bothered to house-train him and he grew too big so was banished to a shed, tied up and shut in.

On a visit to the vet we saw a notice about a 'big shaggy dog looking for a home', so we went to have a look. It was love at first sight, even though this big long-legged puppy was filthy, covered in knots, not house-trained and tied up with a short length of rope in his draughty shed, with no place to move out of his own mess.

We thought he was about a year old, with a noble stature under that messy coat. After a few minutes of looking him over and talking to him he seemed to take to us as cordially as we took to him. We quickly decided he was well worth a second chance so we took him home, put him in the tub, snipped off the matted fur and started the necessary training at once.

Within one week he was asking with a single bark to go out and another single bark to come back in. There was certainly no need for obedience classes; he sensed at once what was expected of him.

On a beautiful summer Sunday when Brigadier had been one of the family for about a year, St John's town was pretty well deserted, with half the population at a star-studded rock concert and the other half, including us, out in the country. Why we left Brig behind I can't remember, but it was pure luck that we did. At the same time, the Royal Newfoundland Constabulary were on what they called 'work to rule' because of some argument with management. Naturally, the local villains took advantage and there was a rash of house break-ins.

When we arrived home we found a window in the front door smashed, with obvious bloodstains on the edge of the broken glass. The door was still locked and we could hear Brigadier's ferocious bark booming out. Going inside we found him stationed rigidly at the bottom of the stairs, snarling with his hair on end – a very scary vision of angry canine. When he recognized us he calmed down and the regular tail-wagging welcome began.

Our next-door neighbour, who had been awaiting our return, told us that some time earlier Brig's ferocious barking had alerted them that something was amiss, and they came to their door to see the would-be thieves taking off down the hill, one of them clutching a bleeding hand. They guessed that, having broken the window, the man put his hand through to unlock the door, but the sound and sight of this big dog bellowing inside caused the thief to snatch his hand back in panic, cutting himself badly on the shattered glass.

The police were called and we were informed how lucky we were. 'There have been a score of successful break-ins all over town this weekend,' they said, 'but that dog of yours stopped them cleaning you out!'

From then on Brigadier was our hero.

He lived with us for another 12 wonderful years. But at the end we knew he was suffering too much from the painful ailments that large dogs are prone to, so with much sorrow and regret we decided to have the vet help him to his rest. It was one of the saddest days of our lives and we will never forget Brigadier.

His ashes are buried under a paving stone in our garden.

John Holmes
St John's
Newfoundland

Kindred souls

Late one October morning a few years ago, the Ottawa Humane Society (OHS) received a desperate call from Annik, a phone agent at Starship Group, a courier company in Ottawa. Their office dog, Emily, a beautiful and gentle shepherd mix, had just found a tiny kitten clinging to life.

John, Emily's owner, had taken Emily out for a routine romp, when she made a beeline for the swamp behind the office building and proceeded to plunge in. A moment later Emily was wading out of the freezing water, gently holding a small, partially frozen, crying brown tabby kitten in her mouth.

Rushing inside, John alerted Annik, who placed the kitten in a box with a towel and called the OHS. Soon, Diane McGee from the OHS arrived to help the hypothermic kitten. His skin had turned a shade of blue and his fur was matted with chunks of icy mud. Diane kept the kitten warm and massaged him periodically to keep his heart going. A few hours later, the six-week-old kitten's temperature had risen to almost normal and he was beginning to show interest in food. At that time, he was named 'Miracle McGee' by OHS staff.

Miracle McGee eventually found a new home and a new name. Roger and Cindy came to the OHS to find a new companion and considered many different cats. But, for some inexplicable reason, Roger's attention kept coming back to that unassuming little brown tabby. Once the kitten was in his arms, a staff member told him about the incredible rescue from an Ottawa marsh area. Roger felt an immediate bond.

Roger's life had also been permanently changed by a severe accident followed by an extraordinary rescue. Only a year previously Roger's car had collided with a moose, leaving Roger perilously trapped in a swampy wooded area of Atlantic Canada. A team of rescue workers had to free him from his vehicle with the 'jaws of life'.

Max (McGee's adoptive name) and Roger are two survivors brought together by fate. They are an incredible example of how humans and animals relate to each other in unique and compelling ways. Roger later told the OHS, 'Now that he's been with us, we can't imagine a more perfect pet, with a more ideal personality. He has brightened our lives considerably.'

The story has stayed with me for its serendipity and wonder.

Eric Adriaans, Canadian Federation of Humane Societies
Nepean
Ontario

'No, not the mean-looking Doberman!'

When I was a young girl of 13, we moved to a farm. My father said I could get a dog. After school I rushed to the local SPCA and looked carefully at each and every animal. I got home and announced to my dad that he could adopt any dog in the shelter except one, a Doberman that looked mean. It was the only dog I was afraid to touch. This caught my father's attention. 'I've always wanted a Doberman,' he reflected.

When I arrived home from school the next day, I was surprised to find a dog in the living room – the very dog I hadn't wanted, the Doberman. She was very thin and a grey colour, which we later discovered was dandruff. She held her head to one side from an untreated ear infection.

Well, a dog is a dog and finally I had one. Trisha soon overcame her fear of me, and I of her. We became fast friends, inseparable. She slept on my bed, and together we learned about life on a farm – a grand adventure. My father later told a friend, 'I got myself a Doberman, but I lost it. I lost it to her,' he said, pointing at me.

Trisha became the dog of a lifetime. We all loved her and felt she understood our every emotion. When we returned home from school at the end of every day, she would bring us a present, grabbing in her mouth whatever was available (often a shoe), then circling the kitchen whining and crying with unrestrained joy.

If we had heartaches, the dog seemed to experience the pain with us and offer consolation. When my rabbit died she laid her head quietly in my lap and even cried softly with me.

One day a large, deep-voiced man came to the farm to speak with my father. The man kicked the dog out of his way in a gruff manner and continued walking across the yard with my dad. The dog watched them for a moment, then, perceiving that her owner was in imminent danger from the visitor, took a run at the man from behind and threw

Jean Epp-Gauthier

Trisha the dog

the weight of her body against him, causing the huge man to stumble and nearly fall to the ground. Of course my father apologised to the poor fellow, but secretly we all felt a little safer with Trisha to protect us.

A dog that ruthlessly killed mice, rats and gophers with lightning speed (at least the poor creatures didn't suffer), Trisha soon learned which of my many pets were friends that she must not harm. Comically, the little baby ducks thought she was their mother. Trisha was followed everywhere. She walked awkwardly, trying not to step on the fluffy chirping brood, and looking confused when they pecked her black nose.

On one occasion, she gently rescued a wild muskrat that had been hit by a car. Somehow she felt that this muskrat needed help and brought it to me.

One day my doves accidentally escaped from their cage. I thought I'd never see them again, yet not long after, Trisha came to my mom in the garden and laid something gently on the ground at her feet. It was a little dove, completely unharmed.

Trisha was a true and loyal friend, proof positive that dogs understand a great deal about humans and are remarkably intelligent and sensitive.

Jean Epp-Gauthier
Saskatoon
Saskatchewan

A real pro

We got our Kuvasz, 'Lofranco's Xuberant Briar', when she was eight weeks old. She's now over 13 and has been suffering from the effects of bone cancer.

Her world is our backyard, which backs onto the fourth hole of the Briars Golf Club in Jackson's Point, Ontario. At an early age she discovered that, if she found a golf ball in the yard and gave it to my husband, she would receive a cookie for not marking the ball with her teeth.

She also learned to hide golf balls all over the yard, where she could quickly retrieve them when the desire for a cookie came upon her. Bill now has a filing cabinet full of golf balls, filed by their brand, colour and condition. Every golfer in our family has always had free golf balls because of Dolly's talent for finding them and bringing them undamaged to Bill. The one thing she insists on is that she will only give the golf balls to Bill.

On occasion, golfers have tried to climb the high fence, but Dolly charges the fence and they quickly jump back to the ground. Bill just has to ask her, 'Did you find any golf balls today?' and she races out into the yard to find one or retrieve a previously found ball from its hiding place.

Sometimes she arrives with two in her mouth and will give up only one at a time. She needs to see that she's getting two cookies for two golf balls. Who says dogs can't count?

Dolly has even been known to grab the long golf ball retriever poles that golfers use to get balls from water hazards. They stick them through the fence and she grabs them and pulls them in a tug of war. She'll then pick up the golf ball and stand, teasing the golfer with it. Most of them stomp away in disgust, but some of them actually laugh about it.

Dolly is a bright dog and understands a lot of words. She loves a ride in the car to buy the newspaper with Bill and recognises the gas attendants when they stop for gas. They always have cookies for her.

She's been obedience trained and I'm proud that she heels so well when she walks with us, ignoring everything else but my husband and me.

She knocks on the door when she wants in. It's not a scratch but actually sounds like someone knocking on the door! Sometimes she will open the screen door adjacent to our deck and stroll into the living room. We've never managed to teach her to close it, though.

The Kuvasz is a very intelligent breed and is happiest if it has a job to perform. Dolly is our second Kuvasz. Bonnie was our first, and a well-known pet therapy dog – a new challenge for an experienced owner.

If I was younger, I'd like to train a Kuvasz to be a search and rescue dog (they'd be great at it, I'm sure) but, at age 70, the dog would soon have a full-time job keeping me out of trouble.

We know we will have Dolly with us for only a few more months. She'll be missed when she's gone, especially by Bill to whom she's been a special companion. He'll miss her sitting on the couch beside him, watching the golf on TV and dreaming about all those golf balls – and cookies.

Marlene Phillips
Sutton West
Ontario

Stay put!

In the spring we purchased our young chicks from the hatchery. They were put in a fenced area within a small shelter.

Every time I checked on the chicks or closed them in for the evening our dog, a German shepherd named Deno, would be with me.

One afternoon we were invited to a neighbour's for supper. It was too early to close the chicks in. I was sure they would be fine till we got back home. As soon as we arrived home, I went to shut the door. Deno followed me as usual.

The chicks were gathered in a nice pile in a corner of the shelter. Deno sat looking at me. She didn't know she should be very gentle. She had killed every chick in trying to make them stay put. Now I am much more careful about trusting Deno with our chickens!

Loraine Anderson
Moose Jaw
Saskatchewan

A personal nurse

Back in December of 2001, we purchased our dog Jade from the Humane Society. She was a mix of Rottweiler and black Lab and had

54

the most beautiful face I had ever seen. I fell in love with her at first sight and knew I wanted to take her home. Jade was the most loving dog but also very shy, and took her time getting to know us as we took our time getting to know her.

In May of 2002 I was moving from my home to a new one and was busy packing everything up. Jade took it all in her stride, never appearing anxious or curious. She would sit and watch me – this was just another day in her everyday normal life.

On the night before the actual move, my son and his friend were helping to load up the truck to make the move go more quickly. After working all day, that night everyone was exhausted and looking forward to just going to sleep. Since all the furniture was packed in the truck, we just curled up on the rug on the floor and fell right to sleep.

Some time later, Jade started to fuss. She was pacing and whining and would not settle down. This was so unlike her, as she was a very well-behaved and quiet dog. My son spoke to her and told her to lie down and go to sleep. She was quiet for about one minute and then started fussing again. My son thought maybe she needed to go outside, so he got up to let her out and noticed she was lying on top of his friend.

When my son got up and went to the door to let Jade out she would not budge, no matter how much he called her. He then called his friend's name and there was no answer, so he called again and still nothing, so he went over to shake him. That is when he noticed that his friend James, who is a diabetic, was having a seizure. He tried to wake him with no success, so he called 911 and the ambulance arrived in a few minutes.

After treating my son's friend the paramedics said that, had our dog not caused the fuss and woken us up, his friend could have died. I had always known that Jade was special from the minute I laid eyes on her but she just proved she was smarter than Jack. She is now considered

Linda Dalton

Jade the dog

our faithful protector and has since, on two other occasions, alerted us when James was having difficulties. James calls her his own personal nurse, because she watches over him whenever he is here. She is not just the family pet. She is a treasured member of our family, and our hero.

Linda Dalton
Kanata
Ontario

Bob's little hero

It was a cold September day when 70-year-old Bob, his wife and pet dog Tina travelled into Manning Park in their motorhome. While setting up camp, Bob's wife took Tina down to the lake for a walk. On returning she told Bob of the path to the lake.

After dinner, Bob decided to take Tina for another walk and chose the path to the lake. It was about 6.30pm and Bob thought a further walk and exercise after a long drive would feel good. Arriving at the lake, Bob met a young couple and asked them if the path went around the lake and back to the campground, and was told it would. Bob proceeded to follow the shoreline, knowing the lake was small, but was unaware that there were three lakes all connecting.

The path followed most of the shoreline, but in some areas the lake was hidden by heavy trees and brush. Bob walked and walked, thinking that certainly around the next turn would bring him in view of the campground. After a good hour and a half, Bob realized it was getting late and the sun would be setting within the hour, so a decision had to be made to go around the next bend or turn back. Around the next bend Bob saw a sign and approached it . . . it was directions to another trail so Bob and Tina started to backtrack.

Now the time was near 8 pm. The darkness fell like someone had turned out the lights, and the path could no longer be seen. The only light was straight up or the reflection of the sky in the lake. Now Bob knew he was in deep trouble, as the path had been very winding, rough terrain with many drop-offs, impossible to follow. Bob yelled across the lake, but no light or reply returned, only his echo. A slight panic came over Bob, as he knew that at this time of year the park was mostly unoccupied.

Tina was on her leash and stayed very close to Bob. Bob bent and petted her and told her to 'Go find Mummy'! Bob often said this to Tina when he couldn't find where his wife was in the yard or in the house. Tina always found her.

Bob held Tina's leash very short as Tina led the way, hoping she would stay on the path. Several trips and a short fall down a cliff made it quite a scary journey, because when Bob fell he lost Tina. On his stomach Bob felt for the path, and Tina licked his face.

Off again, and finally a light from a car at the end of the lake and Bob knew the campground would be near. It was nearing 10 pm by now as Bob and Tina approached the car lights. Many more appeared, and coming towards Bob and Tina was a man who identified himself as a ranger, asking if Bob was Bob and he replied yes. The ranger escorted him to his camper and said he'd better go see his wife right away as she was very upset.

He learned from his wife that she had told the campground attendant who came to collect the camp fee that Bob had been gone for many hours, which resulted in the attendant calling for a search party. Bob also learned that he had walked more than eight kilometres, according to the sign where he had turned back. Tina led Bob all the way back in total darkness. The rescue men had told his wife that Bob would not have survived at his age in the freezing cold, and said if it wasn't for the smart, cute little female miniature schnauzer dog

FIND
MUMMY
TINA . . .

Bob Peterson

Tina the dog and Bob

bringing Bob back, it would have taken several hours through many trails. To Tina it was probably just another walk, but to Bob it was a walk he'll never forget. Tina is Bob's little hero.

Bob Peterson
West Vancouver
British Columbia

The story of my mother

When I was born my human mother, Gladys Gripping, was very ill and in fact was dying of cancer. For many years, before and after my birth, my dad bred, trained, hunted with, showed and field-trialled many Labrador retrievers. When I was first brought home from the hospital we had several dogs, but the really special one was a three-year-old black female. She had a fancy pedigree name, of course, but the family all called her simply 'Blackie'.

She was housed in an outdoor kennel, with dog door access to a small kennel in the garage, along with several others of our Labs. However, all the dogs got lots of attention from my dad and my older siblings and were most often out in the yard. But it was only Blackie that was allowed to sit out in the front yard alone (there was no fence) as she never left it, even if unattended. This was not something that Dad trained Blackie to do. Nor was she ever trained as a guard dog, she was only trained for hunting and field trials.

I was born in November, but my siblings wanted to make sure that I knew the dogs (and were often babysitting me as Mother was so ill) and would take baby Stella out to the backyard for short visits, so that by the time summer came all the dogs knew there was a baby in the house.

My mother wanted to make sure that I got plenty of fresh air, even though she physically couldn't take me for a walk, and so would often take me out on the front lawn in my baby carriage. She thought that since she was out there Blackie might as well be out there too. Blackie spent the whole time admiring the baby, and never wanted to leave the carriage.

One day, a man came by (selling something or whatever) and started to talk to Mother and was meanwhile walking across the lawn towards the carriage. Blackie soon made it apparent that strangers were unwise to be approaching the carriage. She never moved more than two feet away from the carriage but stood her ground, growling.

As soon as he changed direction and went back to the sidewalk leading up to the steps she stopped growling. When Mother saw this she went to the carriage and brought me out to show to the man. Blackie was over there like a shot making friends with the man and so Mother then put me back in the carriage.

After they'd spoken and the man was leaving, he (probably thinking it was polite) walked towards the carriage to say goodbye to me. Well, he didn't get very far before he was again told by Blackie that this was not allowed, even though she had been shamelessly vying for his attention and pats less than five minutes before.

It was that day that my mother realized she could push the carriage out for my fresh air but sit in the more comfortable living room instead of on the steps. So as the summer continued that is exactly what she did, and Blackie became my foster mom, always wanting to be with me and crying inconsolably whenever she was separated from me.

Then one day came the incident which could have been a horrible accident. My mother was sitting in the comfy chair facing the window, watching me enjoy my time with Blackie in the sunshine while in my carriage. By this time I was nine months old and taking an interest in things around me, and Blackie was the most interesting thing around.

There was a car driving past on the road when the carriage started to roll down the lawn toward it.

My mother saw it happening and was trying to rise when she saw the most amazing thing: Blackie started barking and leaped in front of the baby carriage and stopped it from rolling off the lawn. She continued barking, and using her body to hold the carriage until my mother got out to the carriage. Blackie, of course, was richly rewarded by Mother and by all the people who were told of the amazing thing she had done, but I'm sure my mother never forgot the brakes again!!

Both my mother and Blackie left my life, my mother when I was three and Blackie later. But Blackie was responsible, I'm sure, for the tremendous love of all animals that I have.

I spent a great deal of my childhood with Blackie's daughter Bonnie as my constant companion, too. Now that I have lived a healthy life to become an adult, I try to return the special love and caring I received from her by being a foster parent in the terrific Animal Foster Program with the Calgary Humane Society!

Stella Schmidt
Calgary
Alberta

Faithful friend

My parents, Oswald and Ann Stobbs, farmed south of Brancepath, Saskatchewan. They had farm animals and pets. Tippy, their dog, was a constant companion to my dad.

They retired to Birch Hills, Saskatchewan, but my dad continued to farm for a few years. Every day he went to the farm Tippy was with him.

One day my dad got very sick and lay on the ground for several hours. Once Tippy realized something was wrong, he would nudge my dad and run to the truck. He did this several times. Finally my dad got up and got into the truck, with Tippy on the seat beside him. Tippy watched the road and my dad. He jumped down and pressed his nose on Dad's foot, thus making the truck go faster. It seemed to take a long time to make those 12 miles.

Once home, Tippy wanted out of the truck. He ran to the house, scratched on the door and barked. When Mum came to the door, he ran to the truck, barking all the way.

Mum soon got help and Dad was taken to Prince Albert hospital where he had an operation. Mum and Tippy visited him every day and he recovered very well.

A dog is a man's faithful friend.

Doreen Trevor
Oyen
Alberta

5

Smart animals are cunning

The silent stalker

My neighbour used to have a cat with a collar and bell. He managed
to walk on three legs while using one of his front paws to silence the
bell when approaching a bird.

Otto Schilling
Saskatoon
Saskatchewan

The mystery of the mice

A long time ago, when I lived in a farmhouse while attending university, I was given a cat that no one else wanted, a pretty little silver
tabby that had been declawed, named Flo. I wasn't entirely sure how
or if Flo would survive out in a rural area, having always been an
inside cat and without the protection of claws. Flo, however, loved the
country and, in her ancestral way, liked to roam outside at night.

Within a couple of weeks, I was opening the door nearly every
morning to find a small pile of dead fieldmice, five or six at a time,
piled neatly in a pyramid with Flo sitting proudly beside them, her tail
wrapped around her feet, the picture of smugness. I couldn't imagine how Flo could have hunted so successfully without the use of
claws. I examined the little carcasses and found not a mark on them.

No scratches, no bites, no gouges. Flo offered no explanation, just chirruped politely and walked by me into the house, leaving me to deal with her 'gifts'.

I decided to find out how Flo did it. That night, instead of going to bed, I sat in the dark at the kitchen window looking onto the yard, floodlit by the bright yard-light. At the end of the yard was a grain auger, more or less permanently in place to use to fill buckets of grain for the stock each day. There was always a little pile of spilled grain around the bottom. There, about three feet away, sat Flo.

She sat, not so much as a whisker twitching, for about an hour – as did I. During this time, small mice would venture out of the surrounding grasses toward the grain, see Flo and scamper back under cover. But Flo never moved. She was like a garden gnome, rigid and still, staring vacantly. Again and again the mice ventured out. Eventually, after about three hours, they started to believe that Flo was, indeed, some sort of garden statuary and not only scampered about the grain pile, besotted in granary heaven, but were so bold as to run in and around Flo, even over her feet and tail.

Suddenly, Flo erupted! Her little clawless paws were tight fists, her toes curled under themselves into hammers. She spun left and right, smacking the mice on the head with her 'fists' as she did so. She was able to kill two or three in one fell swoop – simply by braining them. Then, after piling them on the front stoop, she crept back and sat, still as a heron fishing for frogs, for another two or three hours. Apparently mice have very short memories – Flo was able to go on a murderous rampage again. Not one drop of blood drawn, lulling the mice into complacent foraging until they succumbed to Flo's quick fatal blow to the head.

Flo was a cat that was truly intelligent and smart enough to know that she did not have the usual weaponry and therefore needed to adapt and come up with a new and different way of fulfilling her ancestral role as mouser. Smart enough to adapt and smart enough to employ the patience of Job in the execution of her role. I was truly, truly impressed.

Linda Hegland
Port Coquitlam
British Columbia

Reverse psychology

My friends had a large collie and had just moved into a new home with deep carpet in the living room. The family were all gathered in the living room one evening watching TV.

The dog was lying on the floor in the kitchen, as he was not allowed to enter the living room. Every time he stepped into the room, the father said 'No!' The dog backed out.

After several tries, the dog turned around and backed into the room leaving his front paws on the kitchen floor. Father thought, 'This dog is smart enough to know he is not to put his front paws on the carpet so I will let him stay.'

Kathy Wells
Sillikers
New Brunswick

You're in my seat!

As a family we were sitting in the living room. Spirit, our ten-year-old cocker spaniel, wanted to be more involved, I guess. He walked around looking at everyone, and then settled on Lorne. He ran to the door and back to Lorne a couple of times.

Finally Lorne asked him 'Do you want outside?' By Spirit's reaction, that is what he wanted. He ran back to the door. Lorne followed and, as he reached for the doorknob, Spirit turned and, as quickly as possible, jumped onto the chesterfield and settled right where Lorne had been sitting. He didn't move as Lorne called for him, but sat there with the most satisfied smile. Everyone just laughed. We all thought he was pretty clever that day.

Karen Hadley
Saskatoon
Saskatchewan

The last laugh

Comfortably, the hunter perched
  up on a tree branch, thick and wide.
Around his head sprouted twigs of birch
  and with a charcoaled face, he could hide
from all those nosy critters.
  His bow and bag of many arrows
he checked, for performance and quiver.
  Yeah – that should do it.
Now, dumb bear, JUST deliver!

While he waited, he continued to dream
  of a bear's head stuck on a maple-wood square.
With its mouth wide open, it looked like a scream.
  Would sure give the guys an envious stare.

Very early every mornin'
  up the tree he'd climb high,
with his hopes forever soarin'.

Very late every night,
down he'd climb, oh so weary,
    oh so depressed and muscle-tight.
Another day wasted up there,
    where was that dumb bear?

His body too exhausted and cramped
    to haul his gear back to camp,
thought he'd leave it there on the limb
    and collect it tomorrow when he had more vim.

Next day to the hunter's disbelief,
    then to anger, then to grief,
he saw before him on the ground
    broken arrows; not ONE left sound!
That DAMN dumb bear, ****!!!

Had he turned and been able to see
    behind the thick sycamore trees,
a bear was there, with a Cheshire grin
    and seeming to say:
'Been watchin' you every day.
    I'm the dumb one? No way.
Yeah, man, I've done YOU in!'

Believe it or not, this is a true story which was told to me by a hunter.
He was upset that the bear was so smart – I was delighted, and had to
write the above poem!

Elizabeth O'Halloran
Peterborough
Ontario

Bubba's porcelain throne

Bubba, a grey domestic longhair, sat poised on the floor of the upstairs bathroom of his owner's home, the cat's large yellow eyes carefully taking in all aspects of his new surroundings. He'd never seen a room quite like this before. The floor was cold and slippery underneath his paws, the smells of air freshener and hand soap stung his nostrils. Yet, the most peculiar thing about this room was a strange white bulbous figure.

Slowly, cautiously, the cat crept close to this strange object, his hunter-like instinct telling him to stay as quiet as possible so as not to startle it. He carefully eased his left paw toward the strange creature's underbelly, the new feeling of hard cold porcelain agitating him. Bubba growled, agitated by this strange new feeling, and jerked his paw back lightning fast. Sitting on his haunches, Bubba tried desperately to figure out what this thing was. It was cold, that was for sure. It was then that his eyes fell upon the mouth of the object – unlike the rest of its stout figure, this part appeared to be covered by a soft green fur. Perhaps he'd get a better understanding of the object if he went up there.

Crouching, his thigh muscles twitching with excitement and anticipation, Bubba carefully leaped from his floor vantage point and onto the creature's fur-covered mouth. As soon as he landed, Bubba could tell that this part of the creature – which was backed by a large square backing made of the same uncomfortably cold skin as the bottom portion – was different. His paws only felt soft material, similar and yet somehow different to the floors in his owner's home. He carefully raked his claws through the fur, seeing if the creature would somehow stir.

Nothing. Well, that settled it. This thing, whatever it was, was not alive. He began to take in the room from this new perspective. As he craned his neck to look behind him, his yellow eyes fell upon a

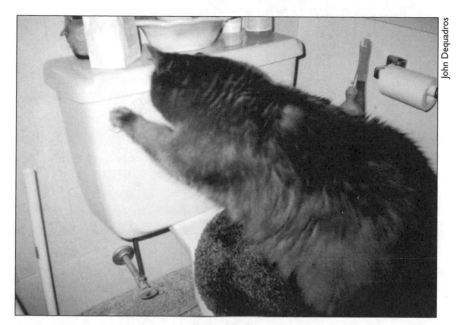

John Dequadros

Bubba the cat

strange white lever located on the square backing of the inanimate object. Immediately, his curiosity perked up. *Something new,* he reasoned. Turning to face the back of the object, Bubba repeated the same slow, cautious motion with his paw toward the lever. When he touched it, he knew this was not made of the same cold material but the same material as the bowl from which he ate his food.

He pushed the lever downward. Suddenly, this supposed inanimate, unloving object roared to life with a thunderous flush. Bubba quickly ran from the awakened creature out into the hall, down the stairs and into the kitchen, and huddled underneath one of the four wooden chairs situated at the table. *Only a matter of time* Bubba reasoned. *Once he quiets down, I'll be back.*

This is the true story of my cat's first encounter with the toilet about two years ago.

During that day, Bubba also learned, believe it or not, how to open the bathroom cabinets under our sink and how to turn the light switch on and off by just inching toward the edge of the sink. Now he has become accustomed to flushing the toilet, and fancies flushing it repeatedly as the best way to get us up in the morning to feed him and our other cat, Black Jack. He will open the cabinets every chance he gets, but tends to do that only when there is an audience present (I think he does it to show off) and, thankfully, only very rarely does he flick the lights off and on.

John DeQuadros
Holland Landing
Ontario

Whitey the wash-day cat

In the 1970s we had a Siamese cat called Whitey who was fascinated by the washer and dryer operation. Every wash-day she would jump into the double cement wash sinks in the basement, and listen to the water hoses coming from the washing machine to try and determine which hose was going to carry the drainage water from the washing machine. I had a suds-saver feature on the washing machine that, when in use, would determine which sink the drainage water would enter. When I wished to save the wash water I would put the plug in the hole of the first wash sink so the used water could be sucked back into the machine to wash dirty work clothes etc.

Sometimes Whitey guessed correctly, but sometimes she did not and got wet when the water rushed into the sink she was in. Apparently she decided her trouble was caused by that darn plug, so one day, amazingly, she pulled it out and left it in the sink. I then had to use fresh water when I came down to do the second wash. This went on for a while. Once I came down and found the plug on the floor beside the sink.

She continued this pattern for a few weeks, until one day I came down and there was no plug to be found anywhere. I searched the basement over, looking everywhere I could think of, but no plug was to be found.

Our boxer Candy, who was also the cat's friend, had a bed in the basement and behind her bed under the stairs was a low wall. One day when I was changing her bedding I happened to look over the wall and there hidden in the far corner was the plug! After Whitey realized that darn plug was back again, she finally gave up and never took it again.

Eileen Ohrling
North Vancouver
British Columbia

The guilty ones

In the summer of 1987 I adopted two kittens, Tigger and Tuffy. They were left alone in the apartment eight hours a day while my husband and I worked. This provided plenty of time for high jinks. I would return to find paper towels on the kitchen floor, toilet paper all over the bathroom, towels off racks and knick-knacks off tables.

What makes this interesting, though, is that lying beside each mess would be one of my stuffed toy cats, there to take the blame. The real culprit (usually Tigger) would watch as I dutifully scolded the toy for its bad behaviour. He no doubt was chuckling at how easily duped I was. Occasionally his conscience would get the better of him and I would watch as he dragged one of the toys to the food dish or litter box.

Cathy Nixon

Tiger and Tuffy

When the cats were two, we moved to a house. Tigger dragged one of the stuffed animals to the new food dish area, and that was that. They were now allowed outside and were too busy to look for indoor mischief.

Cathy Nixon
North Vancouver
British Columbia

6

Smart animals are native Canadians

The raccoon

Fitting emergency

Several years ago I worked at a veterinary diagnostic lab at an emergency clinic in London, Ontario.

One evening the veterinarian on call heard a knocking at the front door in the middle of the night. This was not unusual, as the door was locked and clients had to ring a bell to be admitted. But when he went to the door to look, no one was there. He returned to the back of the clinic and the knocking started again. This time he went out for a closer look. There, knocking on the door, was a raccoon with a peanut butter jar stuck on his head.

Talk about smart animals – he had taken himself to the one place that could help: the veterinary emergency clinic! The jar was successfully removed and he went on his scavenging way.

Jane Neale
St Thomas
Ontario

The truth about elk

Contrary to popular belief, elk are quite smart. But outside of hunting and mating seasons they lead rather boring lives – unless they have a golf course nearby.

'I want to show you something,' my brother said.

I didn't mind. I love the winters in British Columbia's mountains: that breathless hush under the trees as snow falls and the air is cleansed by thick fat flakes drifting slowly to the ground. It was near midnight, and a full moon was bright in the sky. Its light glowed off the deep layer of snow everywhere. Like starlit lamps, it gleamed from trees, bushes and the rooftops of houses and on the ploughed banks next to the road.

We walked down the road to the golf course.

We stopped at the gate. 'Be quiet,' he murmured. The first fairway stretched ahead of us, thick with snow. And elk. A herd of them were scattered across the open space.

Some were kicking at the snow, digging for the fresh grass growing underneath. On the golf course this was easier to pick at than foraging up the mountainside. Each night the elk wandered down onto the uncluttered golf course to eat.

And to play.

A few younger elk jogged down an open fairway. One of them broke into a sudden run, dashing down the open lane of snow. Abruptly it locked its knees, splaying its hooves, and slid for about ten feet. It left deep ruts through the snow, digging up the grass below it. Then, as soon as it stopped, another picked up its run, darting ahead. Just as abruptly it snapped its legs straight, skating along for another 20 feet. Then another of the group did the same, skimming past the first two on the snow-wet grass. Like children on sleds, rushing down snowy hillsides.

Elk may not be able to toboggan like we do, but they certainly know how to use a good thing when they find it.

Sharman Horwood
Yonsei University
Seoul, South Korea

A moment of communion

Our two dogs and I were walking in the bush behind our home west of Prince George, BC, with the dogs a considerable distance behind me. Suddenly I heard a strange scrabbling sound. I looked to my left, and there was a cinnamon-coloured bear standing upright, watching me intently, about 30 feet away. The scrabbling sound was from her three cubs quickly climbing a tree behind her. A more dangerous situation would be hard to find!

What to do? Walking back the way I had come wouldn't help, as she had already seen me and could attack in a second. I decided that, as long as I didn't threaten her cubs in any way, it would be safe to continue along the path right in front of her, as she would stay where she was to protect her cubs.

That's exactly what happened: I kept going past her, and she stood so still, she didn't move a hair or even blink. And it was very strange: I felt a kind of communion with her, almost as if for a few seconds we had an understanding and each knew what the other was thinking.

The dogs eventually came along the path, and she was so quiet they didn't even realize she was there. Once I reached an area where I felt safe, I almost fainted from the adrenalin let-down. But I will always remember that eerie feeling of communicating with a mother bear for a short time.

Pat Stewart
Abbotsford
British Columbia

The following stories are by Hayley Stent and Dene Findlay.

Otters use tools

Sea otters have a varied diet including crabs, mussels, limpets, abalone, clams, fish, octopus and the occasional sea cucumber, but abalone is their favourite.

Abalone is a large, limpet-like shellfish that clings tenaciously to rocks and is difficult to remove. Otters find a rounded stone and hammer at the shell until they dislodge the abalone, then they shoot to the surface to eat their meal.

Mussels and clams are a different matter. To break open the shells, the otter will look for a flat stone to use as an anvil. The otter dives down, finds the right shell, tucks it under its 'arm', grabs a mussel or a clam and swims back to the surface. Floating on its back, the otter places the stone on its stomach and strikes the shellfish against the stone until the shell cracks open. After eating the delightful meal, the otter will keep the stone tucked under its 'arm' and dive for more shellfish.

Is it from watching animals like the sea otter that people started using tools to make their lives easier?

Bears can look after themselves

Black bears in Yellowstone Park are well known for begging for their food from people visiting the park. This is very cute and seems to be a smart way to get food quite easily.

Sadly, it's not as smart as we think. Some of the bears have become very lazy and seem to have forgotten how to hunt for their own food.

But the wild black bears of Canada are definitely smart. They are their own doctors and vets. They get rid of their intestinal worms and bacterial infections by chewing the roots of a certain plant. They also spit the plant juice onto their coat and spread it through their fur to kill parasites like ticks.

The plant the bears use is *Ligusticum porteri*, a plant of the lovage family commonly known as Porter's liquorice root or bear medicine, that has very strong antibacterial and antifungal properties.

Black bears don't hibernate through the winter, but they sleep deeply a lot of the time and don't bother going out much in the cold weather. To make sure they carry enough body fat to stay warm during the winter, the bears eat lots of acorns and fish.

Normally, bears aren't very sociable and often fight if they find other bears in their territory. But when the salmon return to the rivers to spawn, the bears put aside any differences they may have with each other. Large numbers of bears line the banks of the rivers by small waterfalls and rapids and start hooking out the salmon. The salmon provide the bears with lots of fish oil to keep them warm through those long dark days of winter.

Moose swim for their lives

Moose are huge, strangely shaped animals, ideally built for grazing in forests and forcing their way through great drifts of snow. I had heard stories of them swimming across lakes and rivers, but didn't think of them as being good swimmers until I recently read about why they swim.

Moose wade into lakes during the summer to graze on water plants and also to immerse themselves in the water to stop the flies and mosquitoes from annoying them.

They will swim long distances to avoid packs of wolves, often crossing a river or lake to wait on a safe island until the wolves have given up or found something else to hunt.

Like many animals, moose are smarter than we realize and do unexpected things for reasons we may not always understand.

Harvest time

Those wonderful little red squirrels that chatter at you and seem to be telling you off every time you see them are very smart creatures.

When they are gathering their food for the winter, they make sure they have a good cache of rose hip from the wild rose that is Alberta's provincial flower. This rose hip contains a high proportion of vitamin C – which, as we all know, helps keep away the winter sniffles.

Red squirrels have often been seen gathering mushrooms and have gained a reputation as 'druggies' because they seem to be attracted to *Amanita muscaria*, the poisonous mushroom commonly called fly agaric and known to have hallucinogenic properties.

The squirrels gather the mushrooms and take them into the treetops. They spread the mushrooms on the branches and leave them there for a while in the rain and the sunlight before storing them.

Samples of these mushrooms taken from a red squirrel's larder have been tested and found to have no hallucinogenic properties left. This is because the squirrels know that if the mushrooms are left in the rain the drug will leach out, and when dried in the sun they won't go mouldy while they are being stored.

Crafty wild cats

The Canadian lynx is a wild cat with a striking appearance. With its short tail and long legs it is often compared to a bobcat, although the lynx is slightly larger and has other notably different markings.

Lynx often store meat left over from the hunt by burying it in snow. They are nocturnal hunters and will stalk their prey closely before attacking. They are also able to climb trees and will wait patiently in ambush for their prey.

They are generally solitary hunters, although a mother lynx will hunt with her young to teach them how. Then, the lynx position themselves in a long spread out line and move through a field or other open area, and game which is forced to move by one lynx may be caught by another along the line. Lynx are not high-speed hunters; their craftiness is their biggest asset in capturing prey.

Transparent bears!

A polar bear's fur looks white, but in fact it's clear! Each hair is transparent and hollow, and the light refracting within the hair shaft causes the hair to appear white. If you took a photo of a polar bear with film that is sensitive to uv light, the bear's fur would look black!

We don't generally think of polar bears as an animal that likes to fool around and have fun, but actually even adult bears play games. They indicate their wish to play either by standing up on their hind legs with their chin dropped to their chest and front paws dangling at their side, or shaking their head from side to side. Like many wild creatures, their games are intended to improve their survival skills: mock fights and simulated combat, in which nobody gets seriously injured.

Polar bears are also capable of great generosity. Sometimes a bear will ask to share another bear's kill, by slowly drawing near, circling around the kill, then submissively touching noses with the other bear in greeting. If the supplicant shows good manners, they will likely be allowed to share the food.

Salty tales

There have been lots of stories told of porcupines and the damage they can do. They are famous for their quills, which are barbed and cause so much pain. They eat bark and can leave a stand of trees ringbarked to eventually die.

They also often enter camps and sheds and chew on camp gear, wooden tool handles and many other things that people use. The reason for this is to gain the salt they need.

Anything used by people that has been sweated on holds large quantities of salt, and the porcupines will chew and chew to get what they need. There is also salt residue in the glue used to hold plywood layers together.

It may seem destructive to us but it is certainly a novel and smart way to get what you need in your diet.

Clever manipulators

Though at first glance they don't look it, raccoons are related to the families Canidae and Ursidae – dogs and bears!

Raccoons are extremely dexterous, and climb trees with great ease. They can even descend a tree head first, a rare skill in the animal kingdom! They can also fall from a height of 10–15 metres without so much as flinching, and land unharmed.

Their front paws have five fingers, much like our own hands – they even have one finger that is like an opposable thumb. Raccoons are well known for being able to operate door handles and undo complex latches like those on a chicken coop.

Co-operative flying

Snow geese, in addition to being able to walk 30 kilometres when they are only one day old, can also fly as fast as 95 kilometres per hour and make non-stop flights of up to 1000 kilometres!

During migration, snow geese fly in a V-shaped formation, which helps them to conserve energy. Each bird is slightly lower than the one in front, and so they face less wind resistance. Each bird takes a turn at being at the front, and drops to the rear of the 'V' when it gets tired. This means that, as a flock, geese can fly much further without resting than they could individually!

Snow geese are loyal to each other and mate for life; they will only take another mate if their partner dies.

The snow goose has also made a name for itself as the noisiest waterfowl – the main call of the adult may be sounded at any time, and sounds rather like a dog barking.

7

Smart animals prevent disasters

Unsung hero

We had snow on the ground on November 19 in 2001, which was a lot earlier than usual, and it stayed with us all winter. When we retired to bed on Wednesday night, the ice had only reached a little way to the channel to Clark's Pond.

On December 20, Jim and I awoke to find that ice had formed overnight on Lake Rosseau – all the way to Tobin Island and down past Purdy's Point. A beautiful wintry scene met our eyes. A light snow covered the ice. To our horror, we saw two brown figures making their way across the ice from Tobin Island to the mainland. How could this new layer of ice support the weight of two large deer? We got out our binoculars and watched with apprehension.

When they were about halfway across the lake, our fears were realized. One deer slipped and broke through the ice and the other followed. It was agonizing to watch. They were about 700 feet from the safety of solid ground. Somehow, they would hurl themselves up out of the water and use their front legs to break the ice toward shore. What a lot of energy they were expending. We had no way to help them. A crow flew over to observe. Did it offer caws of encouragement?

After about ten minutes, the deer closest to the shore managed to climb out on the ice. The other one was still leaping up breaking the ice, but taking longer rest periods between leaps. When the first deer made it safely to the shore I thought 'survival of the fittest'. However, it didn't abandon its companion. The deer jumped back into the lake and started breaking the ice toward its mate. Jim and I were relieved and happy when both deer made it to the shore.

We wondered why they risked their lives to get off the island. Perhaps they were trying to reach the rest of their herd to spend Christmas together.

Jeanne Pettit
Windermere
Ontario

Flaming grease!

This is with regard to our German shepherd dog of six years. His name was Buster.

After being away from home for the day, I arrived back in time to prepare supper. It was a lovely warm, sunny day, and I had put a pan of frozen grease on the stove to make home-made fish and chips. As the grease was frozen solid, I decided to take a stroll out to the backyard, thinking 'Oh, this is going to take a while to thaw.' Before I knew it I found myself working among the plants, completely forgetting about the pot of thawing cooking oil on the stove.

Suddenly Buster started barking. I thought, 'Ah, he's just hearing things or people' and ignored him. Buster kept barking on and on, the barks becoming louder and louder, and he kept looking up at the house and door. Finally I couldn't stand his loud barking and decided to go in the house.

Well, lo and behold, as soon as I opened the back door smoke poured out, so thick I had to back up and find some clothes to put over my mouth as I was determined to get in to shut off the stove.

I shut down the burner, grabbed the pot of near flaming grease and ran outside with it. The house was filled with thick smoke. I immediately and forcibly opened all the doors and windows and struggled to swish as much smoke out as I could with a towel.

I now know why Buster was barking and acting very strangely. I believe to this day that Buster saved my worldly possessions and my new home. There are days when I have flashbacks of this incident and it makes me very nervous about what could have happened.

Doris Thoreson
Swift Current
Saskatchewan

Guardian angel

Maddie came into our lives at a time when the children were growing up and beginning a new life for themselves. She was one and a half years old. I had gone to the Stratford animal shelter to put our name down for a German shepherd pup. The manager said they did not have a pup but they had a real 'family-oriented mother shepherd'. I declined as I wanted a pup I could train, but I kept thinking of the dog.

I told my husband about it and he said, if I kept thinking of her, we should at least go back and see her again. We went back down and she looked at us with such gentle knowing eyes that we felt we already knew her.

We brought Maddie home and she became one of the family. She was what I will always remember as a 'perfect dog'.

As time went on, we put a dog bed for her in our bedroom. She knew when we went to bed and when we got up, and just seemed to read our minds.

My husband Jim had been feeling increasingly tired all winter, and even though he went to bed in good time he would wake up tired. When Maddie began to sleep in our room, she would get up in the middle of the night to gently hit my shoulder and wake me up.

I would discover that Jim had stopped breathing, and I would shake him and he would resume breathing. Maddie began hitting my shoulder six or seven times a night, and each time Jim was in an apnea spell.

Jim then told the doctor about this and he sent him to an 'apnea sleep clinic' where he was diagnosed with this condition. The doctor felt he had had this condition for at least 15 years and if it was left untreated he would have a heart attack or stroke. He is now treated and on a machine at night to help keep him breathing, and his energy has returned. We both feel that Maddie saved his life by alerting us to his condition.

Sadly, Maddie has now died, but our hearts will always hold a spot for this 'guardian angel' with the gentle knowing eyes.

Joanne Ryan
Seaforth
Ontario

Not that thirsty!

Just before Christmas I gathered some spruce branches to make a wreath. They were covered with snow and grass clippings so I tossed them in the tub to melt. I put the plug in so the gunk would not clog the drain. Then I thought some water would speed things up. I had my headphones on and was listening to an interesting program. I wandered off . . .

I was chatting with my husband at the opposite end of the house when Cline, my seven-year-old giant schnauzer, came bouncing in like she wanted some pets, but she turned away before I could touch her and gave a 'come hither' look over her shoulder.

Thinking her water bowl was dry I followed her. She went past the kitchen to the bedroom. Now I thought she needed me to get a chewy she had tossed under the bed. So I followed on. She went through the bedroom and into the bathroom, where she took two licks of water from the tub which was about to be a waterfall. How did she know to come and get me?

Marilyn Wilson

The smartest dog in the world!

Rowdy was an amazing dog! In his only 11 years with me (due to cancer) he continually impressed me with his ability to assess a situation and then do the right thing and not necessarily the thing that would keep him out of harm's way, though he tried hard to do both. He was a mix of Bernese mountain dog and border collie, and therefore was tricoloured and large, and had the handsomeness of both those breeds.

From humble beginnings as an abandoned pup thrown out by the wayside on a rural road, Rowdy grew into the king of dogs! He was beautiful, intelligent, very loyal, and loved people (especially kids), my socks, to lick out the chicken pot and to lie in his own special chair. He hated thunderstorms, not going with you and giving up the front seat of the truck to anyone!

I have dozens of stories that show just how smart Rowdy was and how much he always cared about those around him, whether two-legged or four; but a few such instances involve him and my sister's old Irish setter 'The Burke's Great McGinty', or 'Mac' as he was better known. This dog lived until the ripe old age of 16 and a half and ran for most of it! When Rowdy came on the scene, though, Mac was already 12, a good age for any dog.

When I first met Rowdy he and I were in about the same shape. He had been abandoned on the side of a road, possibly because his former owners could not understand the immune mediated polymyositis, or sore muscle disease, we later found out he suffered with, and I was grieving over the loss of my collie mix Ted only three weeks earlier. Rowdy was about four months old and had been tied up by my sister's friend so he wouldn't be shot by farmers or killed by a car. After attempting to locate his owners this woman gave up and called my sister. My sister took me to look at the puppy, even though I protested loudly that I did not want to see another dog yet. But when we drove up and saw him tied to that garage it was 'end of story' and Rowdy came home with me and to his new life.

Right then and there I vowed I would never abandon him, and though that promise was hard to keep at first – as Rowdy came by his name honestly and was full of mischief (he once ate both the Webster dictionary and a book entitled *Yes I am a Radical*) – I never did abandon him and I was so very glad!

From the first time he laid eyes on him Rowdy loved Mac. I don't know if the feeling was mutual in the beginning though!

The first time Rowdy saved Mac's life was soon after he came to live with us. The two dogs and I were out in the field for a walk and ran into an old friend and mutual dog walker. I had not seen her in some time, as both her elderly dogs had passed away and mine as well so we had not crossed paths for ages. As soon as he saw her Mac recognized her and ran to say hello. Unknown to us, though, was the fact that she had a new canine companion given to her by her son in an attempt to stop her grief over her former dogs. Also unknown to us was the fact that this lady had been experiencing severe trouble with this dog in the form of protective aggression toward anyone or any dog who attempted to get what he considered to be too close to his mistress. She had not had the dog long and was on the verge of giving him back to the animal rescue from whence he came.

That day, Mac made it to within about ten feet of her when he was bowled over by a creature resembling part chow, part German shepherd and part wild boar. Not being well padded or of great courage Mac crumpled to the ground under this onslaught, and the dog – leaving no room for interpretation – moved in for the kill. It was at this point that a little ball of fur and fire jumped into the fray and straddled Mac's fallen form with his own! Rowdy stood over his fallen comrade's body, snarling and barking and just daring this nasty creature to come any closer!

Though the dog was large and menacing enough to have killed both my dogs he took one look at Rowdy, ready to die for his friend, and thought better of it. He backed off and his owner was able to put him on a leash, apologize and leave. After they were gone Rowdy took a last look around, then stepped away from Mac and let him get up. Mac was a little stunned by the whole experience but otherwise unhurt and we continued on our way.

I was very proud of Rowdy that day, as I'm sure Mac would have been seriously hurt or killed had Rowdy not been there – and had I never gone to look at an abandoned puppy that I needed as much as he needed me!

The second time Rowdy helped save his friend Mac's life was a stormy winter day that had been just cold enough to rain ice pellets and snow, causing ice sheets to form on every parking lot and back road. Then the snow and ice pellets turned to rain that made nice puddles on the already treacherous ice.

I, in my infinite wisdom and because I am not as smart as my dogs, decided after work that I would just drive the dogs to a local off-leash field where the boys would get out for a few minutes and run off some steam and then we would head home. Besides, the main roads were starting to melt off and not that slippery. I had severely underestimated the amount of ice in the parking lot, however. Since there were few cars on the road and this field is in an unpopulated area, I was alone when I made my turn into the long drive up to the parking area.

As I was going up the drive I knew in an instant that I had made a mistake coming at all. My plan then was to just go in and turn around, as there was no room to turn in the narrow drive and it was a three to four foot drop over the shoulder if I got near it. Once in the parking lot I attempted to turn around nice and easy.

Well, as luck would have it I hit a small incline of the rounded drive and the car started to slide sideways. The only thing that saved us from going over the precipice was a small mound of snow that a plow had pushed around the edges of the lot. When we stopped sliding I was very grateful, but it was short-lived as when I tried to go I found out we were good and stuck and no amount of trying by myself could get us loose. It was getting dark and only the three dogs (I had added a second rescue dog – Toby, a Lab mixed with border collie – to the group a month after Rowdy) and I were there!

It was raining harder and getting almost impossible to stand up on the ice. It was a time of no cellphones and the only help was a half mile or so away at an arena. It was getting dark and I had to walk there. I was going to leave the dogs in the car and go phone, but I did not know when and if I could get back in to get them later, and Mac – being old, and upset by my worry – was already starting to panic. Rowdy, being a 'throwaway' dog, was also afraid of abandonment and therefore leaving them was not an option.

So out we all went into the weather. Before we had gone two feet from the car Mac had fallen at least once. When I tried to help him up he panicked, and slipped and slid to the side of the drive where there was a small amount of icy snow. There he hung until I pulled him off and onto the ice again. We repeated this scenario several times and we were getting nowhere fast. I was sweating and puffing with exertion as I suffer from asthma, and Mac was even worse. He was full of panic, hyperventilating, wet through and shivering, and absolutely terrified to move! No amount of encouragement could get him to follow me off the ice.

I tried then to carry him as at least we would then be moving in the right direction, but this too proved fruitless as I would then fall with a heavy setter in my arms at almost every step. Out of frustration and fear that Mac would die before I could get him to safety I started to cry and felt like giving up!

This was when Rowdy came to our rescue. His border collie instinct kicked in and he said enough was enough! He flew at Mac, whom he loved, and began nipping at his heels and hind end like something gone mad. He drove Mac on, never giving him a chance to think or catch his breath. Toby and I just followed them on the treacherous ice all the way down the drive to the road and safety.

As soon as we hit the road Rowdy stopped nipping at Mac and licked his face! Then, turning to me, he gave me a look that clearly said *That's how it's done!* Then we walked to the arena and obtained help. Rowdy may have been working on instinct that day, but to Mac and me he was our hero and my 'Smartest dog in the world!'

Cindy Edwards

Herdsman Brownie

When I was a little girl, about six years old, I lived on a farm surrounded by an apple orchard. The orchard was surrounded by a link fence and I often ran and played with my dog Brownie. Brownie was an old hound dog who let me dress him up, lead him around pretending he was a horse and generally put up with the antics of a young girl.

One day I decided that Brownie and I should go exploring. While my mom was preoccupied making lunch, we left through the gate and headed toward the nearby lake. We explored the shore; I picked up stones and threw them in the water and then decided it was time for a swim. But I couldn't get into the water, because Brownie wouldn't let me. Every time I got close to the shoreline, he stood in front of me.

When my mom came looking for me, she found Brownie herding me away from the water and back to the house. He probably saved my life that day. But he couldn't save me from the spanking I got! And I believe he was treated to a steak dinner that night!

Renae Barlow
Calgary
Alberta

Alarm-cat

We had just moved into our new condo, and our cat Harry (a one-year-old Maine Coon) was just starting to settle in.

One evening during a very heavy rain, he kept running up and down the stairs from the lower level, meowing very loudly. When we could not get him to settle down we went with him to the lower level, where we found water pouring in from between the walls. Without him warning us, we would have received severe damage to our home.

Ted and Norma Seagull
London
Ontario

8

Smart animals amaze us

What luck!

When I grew up we had a very large home, complete with a very large German shepherd dog named Pepper. Her size and breed made her a little off-putting to some people, but anyone who came to know her came to know a dog that was extremely friendly – in fact, came to know that she was really a big baby.

Despite the size of the yard, Pepper was a house pet, more at home inside. Pepper enjoyed having her tummy scratched, and a lot of attention generally. She also enjoyed food.

One of the little tricks that Pepper did was to balance a treat on her nose, wait for the command to 'Get it', and then flip the treat into the air and devour it. My very young nephew saw this trick performed with doggy treats a number of times, then decided to perform it himself with Pepper. Unknown to anyone else, four-year-old Matthew, finishing dinner early, went into the kitchen, picked up what must have been a half-pound slab of roast beef and placed it on Pepper's nose. The problem was that he forgot the rest of the trick.

We walked in on the two of them at just about this time and saw a dog who couldn't believe her luck. However, she was trained to wait for the command, so she just sat there with the meat on her nose. After shaking his head and asking Matthew not to do this anymore, my father let Pepper have what must have been an $8 piece of sirloin.

Pepper also had a taste for home-made desserts. My mother, very

Drawing kindly supplied by Wendy Willett

Pepper the dog

skilled in the culinary arts, is especially talented when it comes to making desserts. One of her specialties is a recipe of her mother's making – butterscotch pie. One Christmas Eve, she had two such culinary masterpieces prepared and left them to cool on the counter-top in the kitchen. Returning a short time later, she found two empty pie shells, licked absolutely clean, and a very content young dog, tail wagging, innocent of any wrongdoing in her mind, with butterscotch-filling traces on her whiskers.

Jeffrey McCully
Ottawa
Ontario

No surprises here

I have had animals all my life, having been brought up on a farm.

1. The animals knew their names.

2. When two of our one-year-old cats, Tiny and Tracy, want out in the sun porch, they know to pull the door open when going out and push the door when they want in.

3. If they get locked out, they get up on the chair and rattle the knob.

4. Tracy is tall for a one-year-old, and last night with three witnesses he stood on his hind feet and tried to turn the knob of the cellar door. He did this several times.

5. Sandy, a terrier dog we owned in the '60s, would put his paws up on the front window and wait till he saw his master coming home from work at 4 pm daily.

6. Our sheepdog Leo sleeps on the floor in our bedroom. Two nights ago, his master was in hospital. He seemed to know this and would not go near the bedroom.

7. Tracy sleeps at Bill's feet. She would not go near the bedroom either.

8. If they are in an area where I have previously said 'No' to them, Tiny and Tracy will scurry down and away. They know that 'No' means no!

Wilda Cudmore
Clinton
Ontario

An act of kindness

Our shih-tzu Dexter is a great little guy in every way. We adopted him as a stray and were immediately captivated by his gentle and loving nature. He later demonstrated his intelligence by becoming a dog agility title holder.

We decided to find him a friend and, after much searching, found another stray and named her Guinness. From the beginning, we knew it would take a great deal of love to overcome her abusive past. She immediately took to Dexter and showed her affection by nibbling his ears and cuddling close at every opportunity. She feared loud noises, abrupt movements, other dogs and anything that appeared remotely threatening. Only with Dexter did she show her playful and trusting nature.

Grooming day came and I gave Dexter his routine haircut with the clippers, allowing Guinness to watch so she would be familiar with the process. It didn't work. When I released Dexter and lifted Guinness up to the picnic table she struggled, wiggled, yipped and tried her best to escape. Panic was in her eyes and she had ragged breathing.

Just as I was about to call it quits, Dexter jumped up and quietly lay down beside her. The change in Guinness was immediate and dramatic: she settled down and allowed me to clip her from head to toe. It was a transforming experience!

Dexter, bless his heart, had realized the role he played in her life and stepped in to reassure and calm her. His act of kindness brought tears to my eyes.

Now Guinness has grown into a wonderful sweet companion and Dexter has gone on to be a beloved visiting therapy dog at extended care homes – his true calling. It is a privilege to be at the other end of his leash.

Nancy Gallagher
Abbotsford
British Columbia

A great team

This story is about Kody, a stray Norwegian forest cat (by my assessment) who came to us and, finding no owner, to whom we gladly gave a home. Kody was a large royal-looking cat who enjoyed the house for his naps, socializing and keeping in shape by chasing our other cat, Smelly. But his true love was the great outdoors; he was a hunter with incredible patience and tenacity.

We live on 50 acres, with the house situated right in the middle of it all. The cutting of about four acres of grass around the house and workshop formed Kody's main area of patrol where the short-cut grass ended and the tall grass of fields began. He would sit for hours at a time on the perimeter of short grass, watching that tall grass and just waiting to see the movement of something through the grass. Once he sensed a possible mouse in the grass, his butt would wiggle and then he'd pounce into the tall grass. Being proud of each and every catch, he would eventually bring them all back to the garage of the house,

Stan Skurdelis

Kody the cat

where he would continue to play with them or leave the bodies as evidence of his day's hard work.

He seemed to appreciate the praise I gave him each time for his display of hunting skills. Smelly was mainly an indoor cat, but when she would go outside, the mouse-catching competition between them was fierce. If Smelly caught one, Kody would make sure to find one as soon as possible so as not to be outdone. Kody respected Smelly's hunting skills but could always display his superiority.

As I was retired, Kody and I were very close buddies, each of us always knowing and checking where the other was and what they were doing throughout the day. One day in late fall I was in the basement doing my seasonal setting of mousetraps to catch those little pests that are looking for a warm winter home. While I was doing this, Kody was sitting on the basement steps watching my every move while I baited and set the traps and then climbed the ladder to place them up on the heating system's duct work, a place away from Kody's playful paws and inquisitive nose. I placed the traps near the edge of the duct work so that I could quickly see from the floor whether they had been sprung or not. Occasionally, due to the intensity of the snap by the trap, they would fall to the floor below with the entrapped victim.

At this time of the year it was normal for Kody to regularly come up to the bedroom at around 4 am and give a quiet cry indicating his desire to be let out to start his daily patrol/guard work. Well, this one morning, although half-asleep, I could hear Kody somewhere in the basement and he was talking (meowing softly) quite a bit, which was unusual. He would talk, then it would stop, then talk a bit more and then stop. Now he was up from the basement and making his way along the main floor, still continuing with the intermittent talking.

Finally I heard him making his way up the stairs, stopping every three or four steps and having a real conversation with himself at each pause. Eventually he made his way into the bedroom. Feeling him jump up onto the bed I instinctively, though still half-asleep, reached out to touch him. To my surprise, my hand closed on a furry piece of something . . . what Kody had carried up and dropped on my bed was, I believe, his recognition of my hunting skills – the sprung mousetrap complete with its fresh victim from the basement three floors below where I had set the traps that day. I think he was telling me *We make a great team.*

My best buddy unexpectedly passed away on November 24, 2003 from a blood clot in his system and we miss him very much.

Stan Skurdelis
Sharon
Ontario

Long live the king!

The sun peeked through the mist on that already warm August morning in 1985 as I sat on my deck overlooking the waters of the beautiful Loch Katrine in Antigonish, Nova Scotia. I drank in the sights, sounds and smells familiar to all lake dwellers.

An assortment of finches, vireos and warblers twittered in the bushes, while chickadees, jays and nuthatches foraged for seeds on the deck. Mister Beaver swam homeward with a scrumptious aspen twig, as a loon called plaintively. An osprey soared high, as a screech drew my gaze to the hundred-year-old pine at the water's edge in time to see an eagle defecate from its special branch into the water below.

Beside me sprawled my black Labrador retriever/English setter purebred cross Ruby, a product of happenstance whom I had acquired as she turned exactly 49 days old from a reputable dog breeder and friend. By age one she'd been spayed and had survived both a collision with a truck and an assassin's bullet that caused her to hold her atrophied right leg off the ground and at 90 degrees to her rear. At age two we both moved to my newly built chalet on a knoll on a wooded hillside facing the rising sun and moon, paradise for us both.

A white calico kitten with brown splotches named Dorothy joined us for our second winter. Initial skirmishes were savage affairs but before long they necessarily settled into a life of peaceful co-existence. Soon Dorothy came on walks with us. They co-operated in the great Canadian squirrel hunt around and around the firewood. They oftentimes snuggled together in sleep and ate each other's food.

Something else changed. Dorothy grew two appendages in her hindquarters. But the name stayed, as did the appendages. Stupid me! Soon she – uh, he – was causing mayhem as he wooed the many nubile young wenches in the numerous barns in the pastoral river valley. He was long, lean and quick as lightning, but he was encroaching on the turf of wily, seasoned gladiators who jealously guarded their harems. Dorothy came home after week-long sojourns battered and bloodied, living to fight another and another day, until after this one night he meowed on the balcony minus the use of his left eye.

My friend Peter arrived about mid-morning with his friend Reggie from Vancouver, whom I met for the first time. They brought 24 soldiers from the 2nd Keith Battalion (21 of whom promptly bivouacked in the morgue) and a certain sizeable, decommissioned old sea captain named Morgan. Pete had his guitar, the steaks were thawing and a time was to be had as three bachelors and the three-legged dog settled on the front deck of the Poopledoop Lodge (Poopledoop: of French derivation, meaning 'shoot the breeze'). Dorothy was nowhere in sight.

Pete brings to mind that 'Pilgrim' immortalized by Kristofferson – a voracious reader, a lover of nature, and I've seen him complete the New York crossword in an hour. It took not long to see that his friend was equally informed and articulate, and quite well able to weave and spin with the best who visited my little house by the side of the road. Both are full of devilment and witty.

At some point Ruby purposefully knocked over Reggie's beer and proceeded to satisfy her insatiable appetite for elixir. That elicited Pete's remark to Reggie, 'I warned you to watch your beer.' That, in turn, spawned hoots of laughter and brought on discussions of smart animals. I proudly told Reggie about my successes with Ruby in regard to the basic commands and the intricacies of dog handling – my abilities magnified and proportionate to alcohol consumed. Before long, she was smarter than Lassie and Rin Tin Tin combined.

I felt compelled to tell him about the time Jim and I swamped my canoe – loaded for an overnighter – in big waves 100 yards short of our island destination, losing virtually all the gear in 20 feet of water. Swimming against a high wind while wearing a life-jacket and holding onto an overturned canoe is no easy task. So I called Ruby and she hauled me to shore. 'Ruby saved me,' said I to Reggie, 'and better yet, Jim saved the beer!' More laughter.

More anecdotes. More libation. Captain Morgan joined the party just as I declare that I'd like to demonstrate Ruby's prowess in the water but it's just too hot.

Later, Reggie, eyes twinkling, asked the question. 'Ken, I don't disbelieve your assertion that your dog is smart. It's five o'clock. We're sitting in the shade and so is the shoreline. How about a little wager? Ten bucks says she can't do the trick perfectly first time.'

I noted Ruby's head on her paws, intently watching me, eyes shifting like Jean Beliveau from me to Reggie to Pete and back again. I wanted to think she was saying, *Don't worry boss, a piece of cake*. But a gnawing feeling told me she was thinking, *Now what did you go and brag me up like that for?*

It was time to bite the bullet, put up or shut up, do or die. It was show time and Ruby's honour must be upheld. We walked down the driveway with my dog heeling smartly beside me and crossed the dirt road just feet from the water's edge. I found not the usual sticks to throw. But I found a remnant from deck construction, a piece of 2×6 lumber about two feet long. Then I spied a 2×4 the same length.

Drawing myself up to my full height, I announced that Ruby the wonder dog would 'sit, stay, fetch said 2×6, turn, fetch said 2×4, swim back with both prices of lumber and deposit them at my feet'. Pete held onto the wager for the winner, just the hint of a smile on his lips.

I issued the commands to sit and stay in my most authoritative voice and heaved the wood far out into the water. I hesitated a good bit, knowing the excitement of that moment for an animal bred for just this task, panting, prancing, salivating, shifting, tongue lolling, eyes as wide as saucers, her every tendon, nerve and sinew taut with anticipation.

'FETCH!'

All owners of water dogs know that moment of the big splash, brute strength and a mind totally focused on its objective. It's man and beast in a partnership honed over time, with a common goal, working in tandem like coach and athlete, a thing of beauty.

Ruby paddled strongly and directly to the stick on the left, and latched onto the 2×6 with strong jaws and not-so-soft mouth. She quickly turned toward the second that she had already marked, turning to see my outstretched right arm as ripples from her wake reached the shore.

As she approached her second objective the wager was looking really good. Then the manure pile hit the fan. She couldn't fit both sticks in her mouth! Pete later recalled feeling in his pocket for the two bills for Reggie but hesitated against all hope. Ruby was stymied. She looked at me. She looked at the two too-big sticks. All eyes were on her. The silence was deafening, we all having agreed that nothing would be said between the initial command and the drop.

Ruby circled the sticks once, twice, three times, her eyes searching mine after each revolution. Then the unexpected happened as we watched in awe, silent and still as cats stalking prey. She released the 2×6, picked up the narrower 2×4 and placed it, perfectly balanced, atop the 2×6. She then carefully picked up the 2×6, swam quickly to me and deposited the 'game bird' at my feet. Then she bounced to within a foot of Reggie and soaked him with the longest, wildest shake you ever saw! *TAKE THAT, YOU HEATHEN!*

Let the animals record that no three grown men ever laughed so long and so hard. It was belly laughs and guffaws and whoops and yelps all round as the money found its rightful owner. After retiring to the deck to replay and dissect the drama we had just born witness to, Pete announced to Reggie, 'And you haven't met Dorothy. Too bad. He's the smart one!'

'You may have a smart cat, Ken,' retorted Reggie, 'but I can't imagine he could outdo what we just saw.' That elicited another round of knee-slapping laughter as the battalion's war of attrition continued. The shadows lengthened as my guests retired to bed and couch, while I sliced mushrooms, onions and tomatoes for the feast to come. I didn't see Dorothy arrive home from his latest primordial foray. Reggie did.

'Pete. Ken. Come into the bathroom, quick!' exclaimed Reggie with a sense of urgency. All three of us crammed into the tiny bathroom. It took a few seconds to absorb the scene before us. There sat Dorothy on the toilet seat washing his face, oblivious to his subjects. On the floor at his feet sprawled one very dead rabbit as big as Dorothy himself. Reggie was the first to react, his sparkling wit shining through. Expression sombre, he went down on one knee, bowed his head and in a very reverential tone blurted out, 'THE QUEEN IS DEAD! LONG LIVE THE KING!'

I don't know nor care if either animal was smarter than Jack. But I do know that the antics of my lovable black three-legged dog and white one-eyed cat provided me with smiles and chuckles all their lives. Ruby never again performed as well as that one awesome summer day. She merited euthanasia on Friday, November 13, 1992, aged 12. She's buried in a tiny glade 50 feet from her old doghouse and the lake where she was so much at home. Dorothy never again brought home a rabbit. He was dethroned in 1998, mortally wounded by a bloody coup. But that's a whole other story.

Ken Purcell
Antigonish
Nova Scotia

9

Smart animals love their food

How did that get there!

Sham, our Old English sheepdog, was trained to not eat anything unless placed in her food dish. This was done because our previous dog had been poisoned.

At age four Sham was very smart – and cunning. One day I dropped a nice still-warm roast bone on the deck away from her dish. The smell must have been killing her. She stood over the meat-laden bone, drooling in anticipation of me picking it up and placing it in her dish as in previous lessons. However, I walked away and observed her.

In the glass sliding door reflection I saw her pick up the bone and very quickly drop it in her dish, then give an excited yelp to get my attention. As I turned around, the expression on her face was unbelievable – sort of *Oh, look what I found in my dish!* Then she grabbed it and started to gnaw, with rolling eyes – she was in heaven.

I guess not touching this gorgeous roast bone was just too much to ask!

John Winter
Langley
British Columbia

One step closer . . .

One hot summer evening Tanya Samoyed and I were sitting on the back stairs, taking advantage of a cool breeze while I ate my hamburger, when ten-year-old Craig came into the yard.

Coming up the stairs, he said 'Excuse me, Tanya' and squeezed in to sit companionably between Tanya and me – and the hamburger. I could see her anxious face craning around Craig, when she suddenly got up and ran down the stairs. Picking up a tennis ball, she stood, tail wagging gently, looking at Craig. 'Oh, Tanya,' said he, rising to his feet and starting down the stairs, 'do you want me to throw that for you?'

Well, he hadn't gone more than a step or two when Tanya spat out the ball, shot past Craig to the top of the stairs and pressed up against me, eyes once again glued on the hamburger.

May McConnell
Aldergrove
British Columbia

The cue

When my Fimo (pronounced Feemo) first arrived in my home at the age of six weeks from the Edmonton Humane Society, it was apparent to me that he was quite motivated by food. It was the wintertime and still dark out in the morning when it was time to feed him, so I would pull the chain on the lamp beside my bed, get up and fill his dish, then go back to bed.

After a few days of this routine I was awakened at what felt like an unearthly hour by the light beside my bed being turned on. I opened my left eye just a crack and there was my little Fimo with the lamp chain between his toes, looking at me, wondering why I wasn't

May McConnell

Tanya the dog

jumping into action and getting his food. I looked at the clock – it was 3.23 am!

From time to time over the next year or so he would turn on the light in the middle of the night, to which he heard 'No!' Then we moved to another apartment and I gave away my lamp and some other furnishings.

We didn't much like the new apartment, so six months later we moved back into the old apartment building. I purchased a new bed-side lamp, which also had a pull chain. You guessed it! My very first night back in the old apartment with a new lamp – CLICK – on went the light in the wee hours of the morning!

(P.S. I don't own lamps with pull chains anymore and I'm much more well rested!)

Jan Walsh
Calgary
Alberta

You'll need this!

In the early 1950s I lived in a boarding house in Ottawa, ON with a fellow who owned a black Labrador retriever named Joey. Because the boarding house was no place for a dog, my friend and roommate Pete left his retriever with his mother on a small farm not far from Brockville. I was frequently invited to go to the farm to spend the weekend with the family. It was Pete's custom to take several cans of dog food home every Friday for his dog.

One evening when we arrived at the farm we carried the canned dog food into the kitchen and left it unattended on a low bench. While we were having a cup of tea a short while later, Joey picked up a can of dog food and brought it over to Pete, and then immediately went to a small open sink where a can opener was kept for opening the dog food and carried it back to Pete also. I was astounded, to say the least, at this apparent 'reasoning'. Pete took the can opener and slid it along the floor back to the sink without opening the can, but the dog persisted and brought the can opener back a second time. There was no doubt the dog understood the relationship between the can opener and the cans of dog food.

The intelligence of this dog later prompted me to own a Labrador retriever when I had a home of my own. Intelligent as he also was, he never measured up to Joey's intellect – a dog who intrigues me to this day, because of this episode and similar exploits.

Although Joey is long gone, his owner still lives near Brockville and can verify this story.

John Marsch
Swift Current
Saskatchewan

Please may I have some more?

I had finished my lunch and had saved just a few morsels for my dog Spirit, a Nova Scotia duck tolling retriever. I put the morsels on the lid of my Tupperware container and put it on the floor for him. Then I went back to working at my computer. After a short while, I was conscious of Spirit sitting beside me. I finally looked over, and there he was sitting looking at me holding the edge of the Tupperware lid in his mouth so that it was horizontal like a plate. I laughed and thought he was like Oliver Twist holding out his bowl and saying, 'Please sir, may I have some more?'

He does the same thing in the car when he's thirsty. I always keep one of those foldable dog bowls in the back of the car. He started

Shelagh MacDonald

Spirit and friend

doing it on the way home from our obedience class when he was a little younger. He would be a little thirsty after the excitement and activity of the class, so he would rummage in the back of the car and find the bowl. I would look in the rear-view mirror and see him standing there holding the bowl in his mouth!

Shelagh MacDonald
Ottawa
Ontario

Height is no barrier

Shortly after adopting our second basset hound, Wilbur, we discovered how smart these sad-looking dogs are.

When Wilbur was about nine months old we discovered that food started to disappear off the kitchen table. We suspected the innocent-looking Wilbur; however, we did not know how he was getting things off the table with legs that are only six inches long! To find out what was happening, we placed some freshly baked johnnycake in the centre of the table well out of his reach and pushed all of the chairs in. The family then hid so we could watch what would happen to the cake.

Wilbur approached the table with his nose held high. He then looked around the room and, after assuring himself he was alone, he went over to a chair and pushed it away from the table. One more circle of the kitchen was made before he jumped up on the chair. Unsure of himself, he again looked around the kitchen and then made the final leap to the top of the table.

It was at this time that the five members of the family who had watched Wilbur execute his attack on the cake came into the kitchen at the same time. The startled basset let out a yelp and jumped off the table, and of course gave us an innocent look as he continued to chew on the cake in his mouth.

When food is involved a basset will do anything.

Gord Drayton
Saskatoon
Saskatchewan

Lucky dog!

My grandmother told the story many times about one of her favourite family dogs. His name was Lucky and he was an all-black, floppy-eared, fuzzy, medium-sized dog with a beautiful tail that plumed out behind him. He lived in the 1940s with my grandmother and grandfather (Ruby and Herb Hammond) and their family in the busy railroad town of Palmerston, Ontario.

During the summers, the family (including my mom, Adele) packed up themselves and Lucky and went to another railroad town along Lake Huron called Southampton, where they had a cottage. Bowling was a favourite pastime, and Herb and Ruth Johnson owned a bowling alley and snack place near the beach.

Grandma's cottage was a good eight to ten blocks away from the bowling alley. The family often walked with Lucky along the beach to visit with Herb and Ruth, to bowl and to have fish and chips or ice cream.

It was one of Lucky's favourite places since he often was able to partake of an ice cream cone bought specially for him. He liked the bowling alley so much that it wasn't unusual for him to show up on his own. (Back in those days, dogs pretty much ran around – no by-laws, fewer cars and so on. Everyone in town knew who belonged to whom.) Knowing this, every once in a while, Grandma would put a quarter in Lucky's harness and send him on his way. When he'd get to the bowling alley, Ruth would take the quarter out of his harness and feed him an ice cream cone.

Lucky was one smart dog!

Cathy Thomas
Calgary
Alberta

Healthy proportions

I didn't really notice that my aging German shepherd/border collie cross was gaining weight. Every year at the vet's for his annual exam, I was told that he really should be a few pounds lighter, but his physical was always performed in January and we live in 'the Frozen North'. His walks are never as frequent or as long in the winter so I didn't worry much about it, presuming that his weight was more appropriate during the warmer months.

Then one day our cousin came to visit and greeted my beloved Shiloh as 'Chubby'. I asked him if he really thought my dog was over-weight and he said, 'Yeah!', like I was blind AND stupid. So that was that, it was now time to get serious and cut back my boy's intake! Obviously, as a middle-ager he just wasn't burning up the calories the way he did as an inexhaustible going concern when he was younger!

I weighed him and heeded my vet's advice, deciding that I would get him down three pounds and see if he looked better at that point. So I gave him just a little less to eat for both his morning and evening meals. I did this for a week, weighed him and found that nothing had changed.

OK, so I cut his food quantities back further, and instructed my hus-band that we must be consistent about this and get his weight headed downward. We also cut out all table scraps. A week or so passed and I weighed him again – there he was, still at a stubborn 55 pounds! Hmm . . . OK, then – out came the measuring cups and a chart; we started making sure we were giving him less and I called the vet to confirm that this was the right way to go about things and that he should be dropping a bit of weight. We started playing ball with him on his walks and trying to stay out a little longer. Then it came time for weigh-in – and he came in at an even 55 pounds!

Well, this was war! We cut his food to half of what it had been and started on a regime of two walks a day, my husband and I each taking him out. We started giving him carrots and ice cubes for treats instead of bread or dog biscuits. He simply had to lose some weight! His intake was half what it had been and his exercise was just about doubled. There was just no way that his weight could stay the same –

just no way at all! Now the weigh-in was a big event. We put the scales in the kitchen, I weighed myself, picked him up and stood on the scales – my husband and I did the math – and there it was again – 55 pounds!!

We were baffled – totally baffled. I talked to other dog owners, the vet's office and the pet store owner. They sent me home with a bag of 'light' food and we carefully calculated what a dog his age, weight and breed should be receiving. We carried the new food into the basement and pushed the old dog food bag back out of the way, and there it was – a little trail of dog kibble from where the bag was sitting . . . I fell to my knees and looked – there was the problem – my bright boy had nibbled a hole in the bottom of the dog food bag and was helping himself at his leisure to as much food as he wanted!

The next trip was to the store to buy a plastic garbage pail in which we put his new 40 pound bag of food. We were finally able to get our slightly chubby mutt down to more healthy proportions!!!

Sue Dafoe
Calgary
Alberta

Going to great lengths

This story is about a squirrel who used to visit us. We would put out bread, scraps, etc on the deck for him to nibble. He also liked the birdseed we put out for our feathered friends. However, we didn't see eye to eye on who should dine on the birdseed.

I usually hung the bird feeder on the clothes line six to eight feet from the deck – until one day I saw my friend the squirrel take a swift run along the clothes line to the feeder to get access to his snack!

After shooing him away several times, I thought 'I'll fix you, Mr Squirrel!' So I ran the bird feeder on a single line away out to about 15 feet from the tall pole at the edge of the garden, too far for a tightrope-walking squirrel – or so I thought.

A bit later I was making the bed in a back bedroom when I glanced up. I noted, to my astonishment, the squirrel had climbed the pole and was heading paw over paw toward the bird feeder, hanging upside down with his hind legs crossed over the wire!

The moral of the story? Never underestimate the brainpower of man or beast when it comes to a good feed!

Fran Miller
Bible Hill
New Brunswick

10

Smart animals show understanding

Joshua's gift

I recently lost my little Lhasa Apso dog Joshua, who was with me for almost 11 years. To my dread, he became sick and changed from the healthy, happy and active dog I knew so well.

Over time he developed the symptoms of Cushing's disease, which include a ferocious appetite, huge thirst, loss of muscle strength and an inability to control his bladder. The most difficult symptom was restlessness. He would bark and bark, pace around the house, scratch at our legs. He could not sit or lie down for a minute. Nothing I did helped to calm him down. I felt desperate.

Before we could even begin treatment for Cushing's, we received terrible news. Joshua had two large tumours. An operation was his only chance so it was scheduled for the next morning. I immediately began to cry and hold him very close.

Strangely, I felt an easiness come over this little dog. He was able to gain control of the torturous symptoms and actually relax. My adorable, loving Joshua was back.

The next morning, again, he was calm. I said a very difficult goodbye and he was off to surgery. In my head I knew he still had a 50 per cent chance, but in my heart I knew my Joshua would never come home again. He died that day.

Looking back, I wonder how I got through those long hours before his surgery, how I gathered the strength. The answer, I now know, is in the heart and will of a little dog I will never forget. He allowed me to say goodbye to the Joshua I had known for so many years, no longer hidden behind a shroud of restlessness and agitation.

Lynn Cadigan
Logy Bay
Newfoundland and Labrador

One understanding cat

One morning in May a lost canary flew in through our open kitchen door. It must have hidden all night in the tree in front of our back porch. The bird settled on top of the fridge.

It was lucky because we also owned at cat, a Russian blue named Cuby. She almost went crazy and tried, unsuccessfully, to climb up the slippery fridge door. After my husband had removed her and I'd caught the hungry bird in a cage from a previous yellow-feathered singer, I knew I had to talk to Cuby. I sat her down on the table on the porch, looked into her luminous green eyes and said, 'The bird in that cage is now part of our family. You have to be his friend and not attack him. He is as important as you and me. So don't ever harm him.' Cuby looked at me unblinking. I stroked her and she curled up for a nap.

From then on she never attempted to reach for the cage, even when it was hanging outside with the bird in it, chirping and singing. She would lie on the table underneath and pretend not to pay attention to it. Who says cats don't listen and understand?

Gisela Woldenga
Coquitlam
British Columbia

Bad mother!

My story begins with my 11-year-old son buying two pet mice. Through many trials and tribulations we enjoyed having two pet mice to look after. Eventually one of the female mice died, and we felt sorry for the other female so we went out to buy a new mouse. We bought another female but to our surprise she was pregnant when we bought her. We decided to keep her anyway and this is where my story begins.

Not too long after deciding to keep her, she delivered nine baby mice. We were told the other female in the cage should not be any problem so we left her in with all the babies and the new mom.

One particular day, after the baby mice reached their two-week birthday, they were moving around a bit now and becoming more lively. The cage the mice were in had an upper level and that is where mother mouse had decided to have her babies, so the new mice had never been on the bottom level of the cage. To get to the bottom level the mice had to go down a tube that would have been much too difficult for the babies – and dangerous.

My son and I were watching one day and one of the babies was getting really close to the tube. We thought 'Oh no, that baby is going to fall down the tube'. No sooner had we said that than it happened. Down the baby mouse went.

While all this commotion was going on the mother of the mouse was in the lower level of the cage, so she was oblivious to all this. The other female mouse, which we had called 'aunty' to all these babies, went down the tube and picked up the baby in her mouth and brought the baby back to their safe nest.

My son and I watched in awe, and I said to him as a joke, 'I bet that aunty is going to go and give that mother mouse heck now for not watching her babies.'

To our utter amazement that aunty mouse went down to the lower level of the cage and went straight to the mother mouse, and it looked just like she was giving the mother mouse a very stern talking to. Then they both proceeded up the tube to the babies.

We wondered what would happen next, and again to our amazement we watched the mother and the aunty mouse start piling shavings up around the hole of the tube so no more babies could fall down it.

My son and I were just awestruck that these little mice could take such good care of each other, and I was so glad to have witnessed what I call a miracle of animal compassion.

Sharon Huizenga
Abbotsford
British Columbia

The crow linguist

The spring that I was 11, my father found two orphaned crows. He brought them home and they became my responsibility. I never realized how often the little guys would need food and, for a while, I was up every hour fixing fresh egg, milk and bread. Sometimes, I'd wake up and find my dad bending over the box coaxing the food into their hungry mouths.

They thrived and grew quickly, outgrowing the box in the porch. I moved them to the chicken yard, where they hopped about with the chickens. Unfortunately, one of the crows disappeared, but later that spring, a funny little chick hatched. He had a twisted beak, deformed and twisted toes and only one formed eye. Cawsey, my remaining crow, became Cheepy's constant companion. They ate together, rested together and talked together, Cawsey having learned 'chicken'. It was a strange sight to see the two, companionably murmuring together as they enjoyed their friendship.

Collette Lacey

Cawsey the crow and a cat

A farm raises chickens for their eggs and meat, and Cawsey (and I) took huge exception to the catching of the dinner chickens. The men in the field loved my mom's fried chicken! Cawsey would jump up and down, up and down from his chicken yard fence post, angrily scolding as one more rooster was caught. He yelled in 'chicken' and he yelled in 'crow', causing some conscience pangs in whoever was catching the bird. Sadly, Cheepy disappeared one day as well – I was told it might have been the weasel under the granary. Cawsey became my shadow as he grieved for his friend.

All summer, he had teased the cats in order to steal their food, dug his beak into ripe tomatoes and plums, and trapped himself under buckets as he tried to steal the peas or beans we were picking in the garden. So we wondered how strong the tug would be as the wild crows gathered.

Eventually, fall came and I went back to school. The days were long, waiting for the school bus. As fall progressed poor little Cawsey would call out to the flocking crows, yet sidle up for my attention. At times he would join a group, but he always came back when I called to him in 'crow'. He seemed to be nervously watching and we wondered if he'd stay or go.

Late October, he had been talking to me on my shoulder when a large flock settled on the lilac bushes by the garden. As they rose to leave he flew up with them, and we watched as they climbed higher and higher. They went further and further till we could no longer see them . . . and he never came back. How we missed him! What a special, rich summer he gave us . . . we've never forgotten him.

Collette Lacey
Caronport
Saskatchewan

The bird, the dog and the light

Here's a true story about my African grey parrot. He's almost six years old and is the most remarkable little guy I know. His name is Echo. He has proven to me over and over that birds do know more often than not what they are saying.

Let me explain.

It was a Thursday night in January. I had recently purchased a laser light and I was entertaining my Australian shepherd Haven with it. I had been shining it on the floor and watching Haven chasing it around for about ten minutes, when out of the corner of my eye I noticed Echo watching the activity with great interest.

I decided to shine the laser on the ceiling above Echo's head to see what he'd do. To my delight he scurried up to the top of his cage and followed the laser. He chased it back and forth, saying *Come here! Come here!* I then aimed the light on the floor. Again, Echo followed the light by sliding down the cage door chasing the light. Again, he said *Come here! Come here!* I was amazed. He actually used the right words as he was chasing the light!

Haven then decided to rejoin the light-chasing game. When Haven was standing still looking for the light I aimed it on his butt. To my amazement Echo changed the words of what he had been saying by adding one more word, Haven. So it became *Come here, Haven!* He was actually smart enough to call the dog over to get to the light.

This is a true story. There were witnesses who were left speechless.

Ginnette Wilson
Ottawa
Ontario

Birthing coach

We had a little skinny stray black cat follow our young son home one day. She was exceptionally affectionate and so happy to be 'owned'. Our old neutered tomcat Beau accepted her without question.

It wasn't long before we sensed that Cinder was going to be a mother. She seemed so small, and as her time drew nearer she was very uncomfortable. She did a lot of pacing, and one day Beau was becoming quite agitated along with her. Her time to deliver drew closer.

She needed some coaxing to lie down in the box we had arranged for her, as we went on with our day, checking surreptitiously to see how she was. Beau was always nearby, hovering sympathetically, sometimes even leaping into the box with her. It seemed endless and Cinder's pain became more obvious. We removed Beau several more times, then went to tuck our four children into bed since this event had already kept them up way past their bedtime. We secretly wondered if this little cat would need intervention soon. As the children included her in their bedtime prayers we reassured everyone, then went back to see if we could help.

What a relief to find that she had managed the first birth and had snuggled up to Beau as he lay behind her, paws wrapped around her, washing her face and the new kitten. He stayed with her, offering all his encouragement, washing each new baby and licking the little mom throughout the five births.

We shook our heads at the instinctive compassion and wisdom this gentle old cat showed. He made Cinder so calm and shared all her distress during that long night. Later, this unlikely 'birthing coach' also took on the responsibility of babysitting as the kittens grew, washing them and curling round them as though they were his own.

Collette Lacey
Caronport
Saskatchewan

Maya's Kodak moment

Our family adopted a Welsh terrier the spring of 2000. We knew that Maya was smart, but had no idea she had a sense of self as represented by images or could react to them.

The first incident involved a full-length mirror; we could hear her 'talking' in the other room, and went in to see her on her belly giving the intruder a piece of her mind! I thought it was cute but supposed she was responding to the apparent movement.

A few months later a relative gave us a calendar with Airedales shown on each month, and as Maya resembles nothing more than a mini Airedale we thought it was great!

The first picture was a 'mugshot' of an Airedale face on. We hung it in the kitchen for two weeks or so, until one morning Maya finally noticed it. She stopped dead in her tracks, sat and began to growl and 'talk', rearing up to get at it! I took it off the wall and presented it at her level, when she then crept up to it, sniffed at it and, to our amazement, looked behind the picture! Satisfied, she sauntered away and never did it again!

Stephen McWade
Vanier
Ontario

Traffic safety

I commute to work every day, about 75 kilometres. It isn't unusual to see a variety of birds and animals on this commute through diverse ecologies from wetlands, farm fields, small towns and finally the city.

This morning, while coming along the two-lane highway, I noticed something with an unusual shape on the roadside. You learn to watch the shoulders for animals that scamper out. So I slowed down with plenty of time. What did I see? A mother duck and a trail of youngsters. She was looking first east and then west at the intermittent traffic.

I pulled over when I had slipped past, and turned off my engine about 100 metres down the road. When there were no more cars coming from either direction, the family made the trek across the road and into the marshy pond on the other side!

Eric Adriaans, Canadian Federation of Humane Societies
Nepean
Ontario

In the classroom

On a bright Sunday morning in Coalhurst, Alberta, teacher Judith Snowdon sat at the sidelines of the Perfect Pooches obedience ring, holding her breath. In a moment, all eyes would be on her German shepherd Tuxedo Rose, but Snowdon had no worries about that. Already titled in obedience, draught work, scent hurdling and agility, Rose had earned more degrees than most people ever would! The challenge wasn't how well *Rose* would perform. The challenge would be for Rose's handler, one of Snowdon's students, a young girl named Kathleen. This obedience match, an afternoon of fun for most participants, was the culmination of a major school project for Kathleen, who had been born with spina bifida.

Earlier that year at Isabelle Sellon School in the Crowsnest Pass area, Rose lay comfortably in her familiar spot in Snowdon's office. Rose played a number of roles in her job as canine assistant to Snowdon, who was a teacher and counsellor at the middle school. Rose patiently modelled for art students, striking various poses while they scrambled to capture her graceful lines on paper. She frequently accompanied Snowdon to her classes, where, as part of the health curriculum, as many as 75 students at a time would practise the proper way to meet a new dog and learn what to do when approached by a stray.

But Rose did more than that. Snowdon also teaches Humane Education, in which students learn compassion and empathy by interacting and caring for animals. Snowdon also taught the basics of dog training: how to modify an animal's behaviour with the same methods professional trainers use. In Rose, Snowdon had the perfect visual aid to illustrate how and why animals enrich our lives.

Students tried their new-found skills out on Rose, and then went home to practise them on their own dogs, choosing specific tasks to teach. Kathleen, however, had neither a dog nor a project.

Kathleen's physical challenges meant she needed the aid of arm-brace crutches or her wheelchair to navigate the school's long hall-ways, but she had other less obvious challenges to overcome too. Social and academic differences between her and the other students left Kathleen too often sitting apart, on the outside looking in. Snowdon had noticed that in Humane Ed class the barriers didn't seem as high. She hoped that an interesting and successful project might increase Kathleen's confidence and make it easier for her to connect with the other kids. But what, Snowdon wondered, could they assign that Kathleen could do?

'Can I use Rose for my project?' Kathleen asked Snowdon.

Snowdon hesitated. This was more participation than the dog was used to and she might balk. Besides, what could Kathleen train Rose to do that the dog didn't already know? And how would she juggle a leash with her crutches? Then Snowdon had an idea: Rose had never specifically been taught to assist someone in a wheelchair. Perhaps Kathleen could train Rose to assist her with her specific needs – like pushing the handicap button to open doors – and to do it only when Kathleen was in her wheelchair instead of her braces. They formed a plan and got started.

Within a matter of days, Kathleen had taught Rose to retrieve dropped items and to open doors. But, as their work progressed, the first snag in the plan became apparent: the two weren't bonded. Rose's attitude quickly deteriorated into *Why should I do anything for you, kid?* And it was hard to blame her. Dog and wheelchair moved awkwardly side by side; on more than one occasion, Rose's tail got run over. Rose would yelp and run across the hall to Snowdon and they'd have to start all over again.

Of course, as an experienced draught dog, Rose had no problem learning to tow Kathleen in her wheelchair. The problem, they quickly discovered, was getting her to stop! On their first attempt they started down the hallway calmly enough, but as Rose saw the familiar door to Snowdon's office, her head pushed forward and her pace quickened. 'Rose, slow down,' begged Kathleen. But Rose was determined. Kathleen yanked and hauled on the harness, to no avail. Kathleen braced herself as the chair crashed against the side of the door and they finally wobbled to a halt. It became a common routine, and students quickly learned to get out of the way when they saw the pair careering toward them.

And there was another problem: a split second after Rose finally pulled up, the chair crashed into her from behind. Rose yelped, Kathleen shrieked and Snowdon sighed. Snowdon's casual thought of Rose assisting a wheelchair-bound handler was turning out to be more of a hurdle than she'd expected!

'It took the better part of 12 weeks off and on for part of every day,' says Snowdon. 'During their practice sessions, I would see them heading down the hall, Kathleen holding on for dear life, brakes on, yelling "Rose, easy, *Rose, easy!*" while Rose, her head down, her shoulders set, doggedly made her way to my office.' It took time and a lot of liver treats, but eventually they learned to travel together, safely and under control.

And the training had the unexpected benefit of raising Kathleen's profile with the other students! She began to enjoy being noticed by her classmates. They started talking to her, asking how the assignment was progressing, or teasing her good-naturedly about hearing her whiz past on another of her death-defying rides.

They'd overcome one hurdle but had Kathleen been challenged enough? The other students in the class reported various problems in teaching their dogs at home. Rose already knew so much; in terms of training, Kathleen's work had been too easy. They needed to take it up a notch and, after a little thought, Snowdon came up with the perfect plan.

A long-time obedience competitor herself, Snowdon assigned Kathleen the task of training Rose to complete all the necessary requirements for a leg towards an obedience title – with a wheelchair-bound handler. As part of the assignment, she gave Kathleen a copy of the Canadian Kennel Club rule book for obedience competitions and told her to study it carefully. As Snowdon pointed out, Rose already knew the rules, so Kathleen had to learn them too. They watched countless videotaped competitions, memorizing various moves and watching for the subtle details that can mean the difference between a pass mark and failure. Training to compete would be her final project for Humane Education; as a bonus, studying the written rules would meet some of Kathleen's English class requirements.

'I didn't cut her any slack,' recalls Snowdon. 'I told her, "You said you were going to do this so you have to make it happen. When – and if – you get good enough I'll tell you and you can go in a fun match."' Then Snowdon added another incentive: she told Kathleen that, if she and Rose entered, Snowdon herself would enter with another dog and compete *against* them. Snowdon knew Kathleen was motivated by the challenge, but worried about how she might be affected by failure. After all, Snowdon was an accomplished trainer and competitor. 'How will you feel about losing?' she asked Kathleen. 'If I'm good enough to be there,' answered Kathleen, 'then that's good enough.'

Kathleen redoubled her efforts. Because they would be competing against able-bodied handlers and their dogs, they needed to learn how to manage tight turns and pace changes from the wheelchair. With the help of a teacher assistant, Kathleen did daily upper body exercises to strengthen her arms enough to handle the workload. They didn't want Rose to be penalized for not being able to change quickly enough from 'normal' to 'fast' pace.

'For Rose,' says Snowdon, 'the hardest exercise was the figure 8, and she learned to keep her eyes on that wheelchair, no matter what.'

But dogs work best when they love their handler and Rose belonged heart and soul to Snowdon. How could Kathleen win her over? Snowdon, of course, knew that Rose's performance depended entirely on Kathleen's ability as a handler, so she pushed Kathleen constantly to improve. Be firm. Be clear. Be consistent. Give her lots of praise. Finally, Kathleen blew up. 'How come it's always me?' she demanded one day. 'You never tell *her* what she should be doing!'

'Well, Katheen,' Snowdon responded, 'Rose can only do what you direct her to do. She needs to have the commands and signals given the same way every time. She needs to have the wheelchair move the same speed and change direction exactly the same each time. She needs for you to be a bit more encouraging and a bit less demanding. When you call Rose, I want to see her run to you like she used to, not walk towards you like it's an effort.'

Kathleen looked completely discouraged but Snowdon wasn't finished. 'You are going to be competing against people like me in that fun match, not against people like you. And that takes more work. You have the best dog, so treat her like she's the best dog and she'll work for you. You are doing okay but you need to do better if you are going to compete. This isn't about marks. This is about life.'

Suddenly, something changed within Kathleen. When she looked at Rose, she saw another creature who got discouraged sometimes. She realized that Rose needed to be appreciated and praised just as much as she did. 'Sorry, Rose,' she said. They'd reached the turning point Snowdon had hoped for.

The training progressed to the point where Snowdon felt Kathleen and Rose were ready to participate in an actual competition, so she entered them in an upcoming event. Snowdon couldn't help but worry – she knew that a dog's performance during obedience trials is always unpredictable. Kathleen said she would be okay with a low mark, but would she really?

On the morning of the Perfect Pooches obedience fun match, in spite of their progress, Kathleen was petrified. She sat waiting her turn, trembling and fidgeting, when suddenly the door opened and a man with a television camera came in, making his way toward her. He wanted to interview her for a special news segment! Not only was Kathleen going to compete, but she was going to be on television! In spite of her nervousness, Kathleen rose to the occasion, answering the reporter's questions with unexpected poise.

But it was their performance itself that truly amazed Snowdon. 'Her figure 8 was wonderful,' she says. 'The "stand for" exam was perfect, the sits and downs were perfect.' The only thing Rose still balked at was the 'finish' – returning to the heel position. Kathleen had to be very firm with Rose, insisting that she obey. 'I stood there and thought, please Rose, please let this happen!' says Snowdon.

And Rose did. When the judging was complete and the total scores were added up, Kathleen and Rose were awarded a mark of 184 out of a possible 200 for their performance. Not only had they passed, they had passed with flying colours! Snowdon's own higher-scoring performance with Tuxedo Rose's sister, Smokey Rose, couldn't hold a candle to what Kathleen had just accomplished.

For Rose, that day was just one of a string of shining moments that would end all too soon. After a summer of prize-winning agility and sheep-herding competitions, Snowdon decided that Rose needed a rest. They'd get back into their beloved dog sports next season, after a long quiet winter.

But Rose never had another summer. When Snowdon noticed that Rose seemed to be feeling under the weather, she took her to visit the veterinarian. After much poking and prodding the veterinarian ordered blood tests and X-rays, but Snowdon wasn't overly concerned. Rose was only seven years old and a strong, stoic dog. It never occurred to Snowdon that Rose could be sick.

But she was. On the first day of spring, March 20, 2002, Judi Snowdon and the students of Isabelle Sellon School lost their beloved Tuxedo Rose to leukemia. 'I received over 200 messages of sympathy from the students, who truly shared my sorrow,' recalls Snowdon. It was a harsh blow for Snowdon, but she was grateful that Rose was able to touch so many lives and so vividly illustrate the value of the human-animal bond.

For Kathleen, life continues to hold many challenges. But no matter what she faces, nothing can take away the gift she received from Rose that day in the ring: the gift of success.

Roxanne Willems Snopek
Abbotsford
British Columbia

'In the classroom' reprinted with permission from *Great Dog Stories: Inspirational Tales about Exceptional Dogs*, ISBN 1-55153-946-2, published October 2003 by Altitude Publishing, publisher of the *Amazing Stories* series. Copyright © 2003 by Roxanne Willems Snopek. All rights reserved.

The enchanting cover photo

worlds premier animal portrait photographer

Masquerading behind the adoring expressions of our most loved pets are the stories and adventures, capers and escapades that have endeared them to our hearts and made them all a special part of the family.

This wonderful new edition of stories about every day animals is brought to life with the enchanting cover photographs by renowned photographer Rachael Hale. Her distinctive images, famous around the world, capture the character and personalities of her favourite friends while allowing her to continue to support her favourite organisation, the SPCA.

Now with the success of this series of animal anecdotes now established in New Zealand, Australia, Canada and soon the United Kingdom, perhaps the best story is that the sale of every book makes a generous contribution to animal welfare in that country.

Rachael Hale Photography are proud to be associated with the SMARTER than JACK book series and trusts you'll enjoy every bit as much these heart warming stories that create such cherished images of our pets along with the delightful pictures that tell such wonderful stories themselves.

Rachael Hale Photography Limited
PO Box 28730, Remuera, Auckland, New Zealand
enquiries@rachaelhale.com
www.rachaelhale.com

SMARTER than JACK® : How it all began

We hope you've enjoyed this book. The SMARTER than JACK books are exciting and entertaining to create and so far we've raised well over US$105,000 to help animals. We are thrilled!

Here's my story about how the SMARTER than JACK series came about.

Until late 1999 my life was a seemingly endless search for the elusive 'fulfilment'. I had this feeling that I was put on this earth to make a difference, but I had no idea how. Coupled with this, I had low self-confidence – not a good combination! This all left me feeling rather frustrated, lonely and unhappy with life. I'd always had a creative streak and loved animals. In my early years I spent many hours designing things such as horse saddles, covers and cat and dog beds. I even did a stint as a professional pet photographer.

Then I remembered something I was once told: do something for the right reasons and good things will come. So that's what I did. I set about starting Avocado Press and creating the first New Zealand edition in the SMARTER than JACK series. All the profit was to go to the Royal New Zealand SPCA.

Good things did come. People were thrilled to be a part of the book and many were first-time writers. Readers were enthralled and many were delighted to receive the book as a gift from friends and family. The Royal New Zealand SPCA was over $43,000 better off and I received many encouraging letters and emails from readers and con-tributors. What could be better than that?

How could I stop there! It was as if I had created a living thing with the SMARTER than JACK series; it seemed to have a life all of its own. I now had the responsibility of evolving it. It had to continue to benefit animals and people by providing entertainment, warmth and something that people could feel part of. What an awesome responsibility and opportunity, albeit a bit of a scary one!

It is my vision to make SMARTER than JACK synonymous with smart animals and a household name all over the world. The concept is already becoming well known as a unique and effective way for humane societies to raise money, to encourage additional donors and to instil a greater respect for animals. The series is now in Australia, New Zealand, Canada and the United Kingdom.

Avocado Press, as you may have guessed, is a little different. We are about more than just creating books; we're about sharing information and experiences, and developing things in innovative ways. Ideas are most welcome too.

We feel it's possible to run a successful business that is both profitable and that contributes to animal welfare in a significant way. We want people to enjoy and talk about our books; that way, ideas are shared and the better it becomes for everyone.

Thank you for reading my story.

Jenny Campbell
Creator of SMARTER than JACK

Submit a story for our books

We're planning many more exciting books in the SMARTER than JACK series. Your true stories are now being sought.

Have a look at our web site www.smarterthanjack.com. Here you can read stories, find information on how to submit stories and read entertaining and interesting animal news. You can also sign up to receive the Story of the Week by email. We'd love to hear your ideas, too, on how to make the next books even better.

Guidelines for stories
Your submissions should follow these guidelines:
- ➤ The story must be true and about a smart animal/s.
- ➤ The story should be about 100 to 1000 words in length. We may edit it and you will be sent a copy to approve prior to publication.
- ➤ The story must be written from your point of view, not the animal's.
- ➤ Photographs and illustrations are welcome if they enhance the story, and if used will most likely appear in black and white.
- ➤ Submissions can be sent by post to (see addresses overleaf) or via the web site (www.smarterthanjack.com).
- ➤ Include your name, postal and email address and phone number, and indicate if you do not wish your name to be included with your story.
- ➤ Handwritten submissions are perfectly acceptable, but if you can type them, so much the better.
- ➤ Posted submissions will not be returned unless a stamped self-addressed envelope is provided.

➤ The writers of stories selected for publication will be notified prior to publication.

➤ Stories are welcome from everybody, and given the charitable nature of our projects there will be no prize money awarded, just recognition for successful submissions.

➤ Partner RSPCAs, SPCAs, humane societies and Avocado Press have the right to publish extracts from the stories received without restriction of location or publication, provided the publication of those extracts helps publicise the SMARTER than JACK series.

Where to send your story

Online

Use the submission form at www.smarterthanjack.com or email it to submissions@avocadopress.com.

By post

In Canada:

PO Box 819
Tottenham, ON
L0G1W0
Canada

In Australia:

PO Box 170
Ferntree Gully
Vic 3156
Australia

In the United Kingdom:

c/ Integer Group Ltd
Unit 1, Learoyd Road
Mountfield Ind Est
New Romney, Kent, TN28 8XU
United Kingdom

In New Zealand and rest of world:

PO Box 27003
Wellington
New Zealand

Receive a free SMARTER than JACK®

gift pack

Did you know that around half our customers buy the SMARTER than JACK books as gifts? We appreciate this and would like to thank and reward those who do so. If you buy eight books in the SMARTER than JACK series we will send you a free gift pack.

All you need to do is buy your eight books and place the stickers from the covers of those books on the form on the next page. Once you have collected eight stickers, complete your details on the form, cut out the page and post it to us. We will then send you your SMARTER than JACK gift pack. Feel free to photocopy this form – that will save cutting a page out of the book.

Do you have a dog or a cat? You can choose from either a cat or dog gift pack. Just indicate your preference.

If this book does not have a sticker on the front and you have received it as a gift, the person who bought it for you may have removed the sticker so that they can get their free gift pack.

Please only remove the sticker from the cover once you have purchased or received the book.

Note that the contents of the SMARTER than JACK gift pack will vary from country to country, but may include:
- ➤ The SMARTER than JACK mini Collector Series
- ➤ SMARTER than JACK greeting cards, set of four
- ➤ Small packet of pet food
- ➤ Pet toy
- ➤ Books in the SMARTER than JACK series

Place your stickers here:

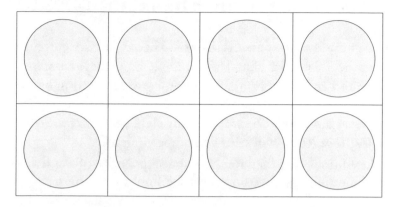

Complete your details:

Name: _____

Address: _____

City: _____

State and code: _____

Country: _____

Telephone: _____

Email address: _____

Would you like a cat or dog gift pack?   Cat/dog

Post the completed page to us:

In Canada: PO Box 819, Tottenham, ON, LOG1W0, Canada
In Australia: PO Box 170, Ferntree Gully, Vic 3156, Australia
In New Zealand
and rest of world: PO Box 27003, Wellington, New Zealand

Please allow up to four weeks for delivery.

Buy a book

On the next few pages are details of the books that are currently available in the SMARTER than JACK series. To purchase a book you can either go to your local bookstore or order using the form below.

How much are the books?

All the editions cost the same, but the actual price of the series varies from country to country.

New Zealand and Australia $19.95 including GST
Canada $17.95 plus GST
United Kingdom £7.99 including VAT
United States $11.95 plus taxes

How your purchase will help animals

The Royal New Zealand SPCA, RSPCA Australia, and the Canadian Federation of Humane Societies and their member societies will receive half of the retail price for each book ordered from these organisations by post or half the profit from bookstore sales.

Order by mail

To order by mail please follow the five easy steps overleaf.

1. Write your details here

Name: _____

Address: _____

City: _____

State and code: _____

Country: _____

Telephone: _____

Email address: _____

2. Indicate the books you want

Book	Quantity	Subtotal
New Zealand animals are SMARTER than JACK 1		
New Zealand animals are SMARTER than JACK 2		
Australian animals are SMARTER than JACK 1		
Australian animals are SMARTER than JACK 2		
Canadian animals are SMARTER than JACK 1		
Why animals are SMARTER than US		

Subtotal for order: _____

Packaging and post: $5.00

3. Work out the total to pay

Total: _____

4. Choose the payment method

There are two ways you can pay:

> By cheque written out and posted to one of the organisations listed below *or*

> By filling in the credit card details below.

Card: Visa/MasterCard

Card number: ☐☐☐☐ ☐☐☐☐ ☐☐☐☐ ☐☐☐☐

Name on card: _____ Expiry date: ☐☐/☐☐

5. Send us your order

Post your order to your nearest society at the address below.

If you are ordering by mail order, note that some of the books are only available in certain countries. If you live outside the countries where they are available, please request the books from your local bookstore.

In Canada:

Canadian Federation of
Humane Societies
102-30 Concourse Gate
Ottawa, ON
K2E 7V7

In New Zealand:

Royal New Zealand SPCA
PO Box 15349
New Lynn
Auckland 1232

Rest of world:

SMARTER than JACK
PO Box 27003
Wellington
New Zealand

In Australia:

Australian Capital Territory
RSPCA ACT
PO Box 3082
Weston Creek ACT 2611

New South Wales
RSPCA NSW
201 Rookwood Road
Yagoona NSW 2199

Victoria
RSPCA Burwood East
3 Burwood Hwy
Burwood East VIC 3151

Tasmania
RSPCA Tasmania
PO Box 749
Kings Meadows TAS 7249

South Australia
RSPCA SA
GPO Box 2122
Adelaide SA 5001

Western Australia
RSPCA WA
PO Box 3147
Malaga WA 6945

Northern Territory
RSPCA NT
PO Box 40034
Casuarina NT 0811

Queensland
RSPCA Queensland
PO Box 6177
Fairfield Gardens QLD 4103

Purchase from your local bookstore

Your local bookstore should have the editions you want, or if not, be able to order them for you. If they can't get the books, the publisher Avocado Press can be contacted direct by email at: orders@avocadopress.com or by mail: PO Box 27003, Wellington, New Zealand.

Order online

Please use the submission form at www.smarterthanjack.com.

Why animals are SMARTER than US

ISBN 0-9582457-5-4   128 pages, 148mm x 210mm, paperback
Foreword by Dr Andrew Whiteside   Released October 2004

Animals are smarter than us – we've got the proof!
This heart-warming and humorous book of true stories will convince you
that animals can read minds, sense the paranormal, foretell the future, sense
distant intentions, navigate without maps, fix their own medical problems
and communicate in mysterious ways. Humans, of course, cannot do these
things!

The true stories in this international edition in the SMARTER than JACK
series are from around the world.

For each book ordered in their country by post, the Royal New Zealand
SPCA, RSPCA Australia, and the Canadian Federation of Humane Societies
and their member societies will receive half of the retail price.

This book is only available by mail order in Australia, New Zealand and
Canada. If you live outside these countries, please request this title from your
local bookstore.

Australian animals are

SMARTER than JACK®1

ISBN 0-9582571-2-4   160 pages, 210mm x 148mm, paperback
Foreword by Kerri-Anne Kennerley   Originally released October 2003

In October 2003 SMARTER than JACK was launched in Australia in partnership with RSPCA Australia. So far over A$60,000 has been raised from this book to help animals.

> *'I have worked closely with animals for over 40 years and their intelligence has never ceased to amaze me. When you read this book you will be amazed too. You'll look at animals with renewed respect and admiration.'*
>
> Dr Hugh J Wirth, AM, President, RSPCA Australia

Distributed by Wakefield Press, www.wakefieldpress.com.au. Created in partnership with RSPCA Australia www.rspca.org.au.

RSPCAs in Australia will receive half of the retail price for each book ordered by post or half the profit from bookstore sales in Australia.

This book is only available by mail order in Australia. If you live outside Australia, please request this title from your local bookstore.

Australian animals are

SMARTER than JACK®2

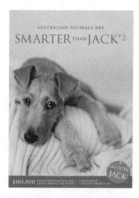

ISBN 0-9582457-7-0   160 pages, 210mm x 148mm, paperback
Foreword by Caroline Girdlestone   Released October 2004

This is the second Australian edition in this popular series. It has all-new true stories of encounters with smart animals, submitted by people throughout Australia. Included is a chapter on unique Australian animals.

> *'I thoroughly enjoyed SMARTER than JACK and was thrilled that RSPCA Australia played a part in this ground-breaking book series. The books have helped to show people just how smart animals are and this one is no exception. RSPCAs in Australia have also benefited by over A$60,000 from sales of the first edition!'*
>
> Dr Hugh J Wirth, AM, President, RSPCA Australia

Distributed by Wakefield Press, www.wakefieldpress.com.au. Created with RSPCA Australia www.rspca.org.au.

RSPCAs in Australia will receive half of the retail price for each book ordered by post or half the profit from bookstore sales in Australia.

This book is only available by mail order in Australia. If you live outside Australia, please request this title from your local bookstore.

New Zealand animals are
SMARTER than JACK®2

ISBN 0-9582571-1-6   160 pages, 210mm x 148mm, paperback
Foreword by Gary McCormick   Originally released September 2003

In 2003, the second New Zealand book – originally titled SMARTER than JILL – was launched. This best-seller has helped raise over NZ$45,000 for the Royal New Zealand SPCA.

> 'Best-seller SMARTER than JACK delighted and inspired readers and resulted in a donation of over $43,000 to the SPCA. It was a welcome boost to our funding. When we read the stories for SMARTER than JILL we were sure this book would be even more popular and we are glad to again be involved.'
>
> Peter Mason, SPCA National President

Distributed to the book trade by Addenda, www.addenda.co.nz. Created with the Royal New Zealand SPCA, www.rnzspca.org.nz.

The Royal New Zealand SPCA will receive half of the retail price for each book ordered by post.

This book is only available by mail order in New Zealand. If you live outside New Zealand, please request this title from your local bookstore.